Amy

Dreams become hopes,
Hopes become reality.
Never stop dreaming.
Dennis + Deepak

From Maggie's letter to me:

Late February 1967

Wouldn't it be something if someday (2 centuries from now) someone discovered our letters to each other and wrote a novel about us? Maybe even an opera. Would you believe a science fiction movie??????

Wouldn't It Be Something

By

Dennis F. Depcik

INFINITY PUBLISHING

ISBN 978-0-7414-9751-2 Paperback
ISBN 978-0-7414-9752-9 eBook
Library of Congress Control Number: 2013912483

Printed in the United States of America

Published March 2014

INFINITY PUBLISHING
1094 New DeHaven Street, Suite 100
West Conshohocken, PA 19428-2713
Toll-free (877) BUY BOOK
Local Phone (610) 941-9999
Fax (610) 941-9959
Info@buybooksontheweb.com
www.buybooksontheweb.com

In memory of Mary Margaret (Brown) Depcik, my Maggie, who taught me the beauty of loving someone without reservations, the power of a smile, the value of the simple pleasures in life, and the honesty of writing what you feel.

Dedicated to my children, Mike, Jenny, Erica, and Paul who will never forget their mother, for she is a part of each one of them and they are more talented, more humble, and more giving because of her.

And to our seven grandchildren (Danny, Michael, Carter, Alex, Olivia Henry and Nora) who were too young to remember what a wonderful grandmother they had, but who will know her through the loving care of their parents.

Acknowledgements

Thank you to all who have helped make this a better book, with special thanks to Virginia C. Foley, Linda Lamb, and Joanne Monaghan.

Author's Note

This book does not contain all the letters written between Maggie and me:

- The letters I sent during the nine-month period from October 10, 1966 to mid-July 1967 were not among those found. Whether Maggie lost them in one of her moves or threw them away is not known.
- A few letters of mine and Maggie's after mid-July 1967 are missing.
- I intentionally excluded several of my letters because, quite frankly, they were too long, too boring, or both.

Of the letters included in the book, I deleted partial segments of some. I did so when that segment was irrelevant to the development of Maggie's and my relationship.

The letters are transcribed *as written,* including punctuation, spelling, grammar, and structural errors.

The narrative and dialogue that precede or follow the letters are recalled to the best of my recollection.

Mary Brown (on right) and my sister, Nancy, as bridesmaids at the wedding of my brother, Leo, and Mary Brown's sister, Patsy.

I can't remember the first time I noticed Mary Brown. I had obviously been in the same room with her a number of times, but I can't remember noticing her.

She must have been at her mother's funeral. I know I was there because my brother, Leo, was engaged to Mary Brown's sister, Patsy, and their wedding was set to happen in three weeks. So, I was there at Mary Brown's mother's funeral and I'm sure so was Mary Brown. But I was 20 and she was only 13, just a kid to me—an insignificant kid.

I can't remember her at my brother's wedding, just three weeks after the funeral. I was a groomsman and Mary Brown was one of the bridesmaids. I'm certain of that because I have a picture of her and my 12-year-old sister, Nancy, who was also a bridesmaid, sitting at a table smiling into the camera. So, I'm sure she was there. I just can't remember her.

It wasn't at a family function. Now that our families were connected because my brother and her sister were married, we must have crossed each other's paths at holiday get-togethers—maybe Christmas, maybe a Fourth of July picnic. But when I recall those times, Mary Brown doesn't come to mind.

I vaguely remember Mary Brown visiting her sister, who lived with my brother in the flat above my parents. She was rushing up the back stairs while our dog, Daisy, barked menacingly. She flashed a smile then quickened her pace before Daisy could get any closer. I can't say I really noticed her. I mean, not in the sense that she stood out in any special way. She was just a cute kid with a nice smile. I was 22 and she was 15. She meant nothing to me.

She wrote some letters to me when I was in Boot Camp and Advanced Infantry Training. I never saved them, except for one. They didn't mean much to me, my sister-in-law's kid sister sending some letters to her sister's brother-in-law who was in the service, just a nice thing to do. I certainly don't remember the contents of those letters, except for the one I saved. I must have written back, out of courtesy, but I don't remember doing so. I was 24 and Mary Brown was 17, still in high school.

Still, Mary Brown continued to write and I continued to answer, and in the course of writing to each other over three years, everything changed. Mary Brown became far more than just a kid. She became my life.

No, I can't remember the first time I noticed Mary Brown, but I'll forever remember the last time I saw her. She was Mary Depcik, my Maggie. She died at our home at 9:50 Sunday morning, November 14, 2010, after 41 years, 2 months, 20 days, 9 hours, and 50 minutes of marriage.

Her life ended.

My life stopped.

CHAPTER 1

DISCOVERING THE LETTERS

It's been a month since Maggie passed away and I'm missing her more now than I did the first couple of weeks after her death, when my days were filled with phone calls, lunches with friends and visits from family. Now it seems this house gets quieter every day. I never realized how heavily our dog, Casey, breathes, nor the rhythmic beat of the washing machine that Maggie said sounded like an MRI, nor the creak in the floor as you enter the family room. Everything seems much louder—and so much lonelier.

I need to be close to Maggie today. I believe she's near me all the time, but today I need to know for sure. Not just in my head; no, I need to feel her, see her, smell her—make her part of me.

I go to our bedroom and sit on Maggie's side of the bed for a couple minutes, slowly brushing my left hand across her pillow. When I rise to smooth the bedspread, I glimpse Maggie's stuffed animals sitting on the headboard—the little brown bear and curly white lamb. I lift and hug them, then place them back where they were. On the other side of the bed, draped over the edge of the headboard, hang plastic beaded necklaces given to Maggie by one of our grandchildren—simple gifts she cherished.

I stand motionless for a few seconds in the center of the room, seeing Maggie everywhere I turn. I walk to her dresser that sits beneath the windows overlooking our front yard, to touch what she has placed there. I have passed these items every day but have paid little attention to them:

> Two music boxes: one, a small blue wooden box adorned on the lid with a single painted flower, and the other, a larger black enameled box embossed with golden butterflies and white daisies. I wind both and lift the lid of each. The first plays *There Is Love*, the other *Hero*. I listen to the music for a few seconds, close the lids, and return them to the spaces where they have probably sat for years.
>
> A small round glass bowl filled with fragranced petals, topped with a gold cover and a gold prism-winged butterfly that shines rainbow beams with the rising sun. I turn the butterfly to catch the rays and watch the beams dance on the ceiling as Maggie sometimes did.
>
> An octagonal-shaped cut-glass jewelry case with a single rose etched on top and gold edges on the sides. There are pearls inside, but I don't think they're real. Maggie once showed me how to test if a pearl was genuine—something about rubbing the pearl across your front teeth. I don't remember what I'm supposed to be looking for, but I rub them anyway then place them back in the jewelry case.

I walk into the bathroom and see one of Maggie's favorite fragrances, Moonlight Path, in the left corner of the sink along with others she seldom used. I pick up Moonlight Path, spray it in the air then quickly walk through to wear Maggie's scent.

I re-enter the bedroom and continue to look at everything that is Maggie. I sit at her vanity table that she bought at a garage sale. On top are a mirrored tray with small bottles of perfume carefully displayed, several little heart-shaped porcelain containers filled with buttons and other little necessities, a silver-handled mirror and brush set I had bought as an anniversary gift fifteen years ago, and a frosted crystal statue of the Blessed Mother and Child I had sent her when I was stationed in Germany and we were just beginning to know each other.

To the left of the vanity is Maggie's closet. I open it and look at her blouses, pants, sweaters, and dresses neatly hanging, some still with store tags. I push all the garments to the far right, then one by one move each to the other end to see what is there. I select one of Maggie's favorite dresses and hold it at arm's length—picturing her wearing it. I gather it in my hands, bring it to my face to inhale her perfume and then return it to the closet. As I step back to get a fuller view of Maggie's clothes, I look at the shelf above.

There are a variety of items that I remove, one by one. Among them are: the *Instruction Manual for Braille Transcribing,* that Maggie used to learn Braille to help our son, Mike, with his homework; *A Bride's Scrapbook,* a wedding shower gift with yellowed and tattered pages of pictures cut from magazines highlighting pivotal moments in a new bride's life; and a well-worn biographical picture album entitled *This Is Your Life,* that Maggie made for her father, Papa, to chronicle his life from birth to retirement from Acme Steel and the years following. I examine each item closely before replacing each one back in its original spot.

In the far right corner of the shelf are a number of boxes of varying shapes and colors. One catches my eye—it's the longest and sticks out three inches beyond the shelf. I begin sliding it from the other boxes and see it's emblazoned on top with "Neiman Marcus" in large silver letters. How it got there, I don't know, since Neiman Marcus is not a store we frequented. The only time we were in Neiman Marcus was to pass through on the way to Sears.

It's slightly heavy and its weight shifts as the contents move from back to front, nearly knocking the box from my hands. Steadying it, I lower the box, place it on the bed, and slowly open it. I'm startled to find a treasure I never expected. It's filled with letters—letters Maggie and I wrote to each other when I was in the Army. These are the letters that seeded our love, growing from her seventeen-year-old school girl crush and my guarded reluctance to admit my feelings, to a devotion that stayed strong for over forty-one years.

I had forgotten about these letters. I remember saving many of the ones Maggie had sent me, since I was somewhat of a hoarder, but I didn't know Maggie saved and kept the ones I had sent her. But here they are.

I'm momentarily stunned—unnerved by their very sight, eager to open, but reluctant to read them. I remember Maggie's letters being alive and revealing; mine, I remember being cautious and boring. I lift a couple letters from the box—one of Maggie's in an envelope and one of mine without. I remove Maggie's letter, unfold it, and am immediately shaken by her handwriting. I quickly place it back in its envelope. I can't read her letters now. I just can't.

Yet, I want Maggie to be near and I know reading her letters will bring her to me. But I'm afraid—afraid to see Maggie's handwriting, read her words, hear her thoughts, feel her love—afraid to feel the hurt, to face the reality that Maggie is no longer here. Maybe if I start with one of my letters, I could ease myself into reading Maggie's. After all, I know what to expect. It's my letter and it's surely going to be a complete bore. I unfold it and begin reading. Although it is my letter and my words, my chest tightens and I begin breathing deeply as tears fill my eyes. I quickly put the letter back in the box before completing the first page, place the box back on the closet shelf and hurry from the room. It's too soon.

Several weeks pass before I can bring myself to try again. With trembling hands, I slide the box from the shelf, bring it to the bed, and slowly open it. I gaze at the envelopes, move my fingers across the tops, gently fan them apart, and carefully lift several of Maggie's letters from the box. My eyes fix again on her handwriting. Maggie's handwriting is so expressive of the soft, flowing, distinctive, elegant, yet unpretentious person she was. I caress the letters and bring them to my face, hoping I can smell Maggie's perfume. How silly to hope a scent might still remain after forty-five years. I think there is a faint fragrance, but I'm sure it's just my imagination. I slowly move the letters from my face but keep staring at them. I still can't bring myself to open Maggie's letters.

I know now that I must start with my letters and read all of them before daring to read Maggie's. My letters are interspersed between hers and are neither dated nor in envelopes. As I begin reading my letters, I don't feel the pain I did weeks before. My initial recollections are quickly confirmed—my letters are stilted and stumble from my head. I remember Maggie's letters always carrying a piece of her heart. What a pompous ass I used to be. If our letters were how we connected, how did Maggie fall in love with me?

I assume all the letters are in chronological order, but it is quickly apparent, from the content of six or seven of mine, that they aren't. Since almost all of Maggie's letters remain in their postmarked envelopes, I soon realize I will have to use hers as a base to recapture the development of our relationship. I can no longer delay reading Maggie's letters.

I lift several of them from the box. Anticipating what I am about to find, I take a deep breath. My heart races, my hands tremble, my eyes mist. Again, I begin to put the letters down—but I know I can't. I can no longer postpone the inevitable. Realizing I can't escape, I begin reading.

Reading Maggie's letters is much harder. God, she writes such beautiful letters—full of energy, life, humor, wit, and love. It's as if we're sitting next to each other having a conversation, as if we're on a date. She's by my side every time I read one. It isn't words on a page—it's her voice in my ears, her face in front of mine, her laughter and her smile. As I read her letters, I am with her again—with my vibrant, funny, loving Miss Maggathie. I cry and have to stop a number of times. After reading six letters, I quit. The pain is too intense. I return the letters back to the closet.

Still, I'm drawn to the letters every day. If I'm out of the house on an errand, visiting one of my children, or simply doing housework, I feel this compulsion to read Maggie's letters. I get anxious whenever I'm away from them for any length of time and feel like a nervous teenager with a crush whenever I sit to read one. It's as if Maggie and I are young again, but my feelings are so much more intense because they are matured by the passage of time.

Yet I can't read but a few a day because the pain is too strong. They bring Maggie too close—too close at the time I miss her most. I didn't fully realize what I had then, when we were young, but now her death has taken me by my shoulders, shaken me and slapped me in the face to awaken me to the treasure I had.

***

About two months after Maggie's funeral, I meet with my sister, Nancy, to spend a day in Chicago. It's a cold, crisp day as a strong wind blows through the cavernous streets and small eddies of snow dance around us as we walk the five blocks from the train station to downtown. I haven't seen Nancy since the funeral and it's good to be with her, to talk to someone other than my kids about my feelings after Maggie's death. Friends and other family members seem uncomfortable when I mention Maggie, but Nancy and I have had several long conversations on the phone prior to this meeting and I know she's open to letting me talk. And I have to talk about Maggie.

Our destination is the Art Institute. Nancy's probably thinking it's to see the displays, but I simply want a quiet place to talk about Maggie to someone I know will really listen. During the entire walk to the Art Institute and the couple hours we're there, I talk about Maggie incessantly. I tell Nancy about the letters, how I'm drawn to them and how difficult it is to read them.

"Why are you doing this now?" she asks.

"What do you mean?"

"Why are you reading these letters now, when it hurts so much? Why don't you wait a couple months when the pain isn't this intense?"

"I don't know. I just feel I have to."

She cocks her head to the right and shrugs her shoulder.

"Okay, I was just wondering why you would do that to yourself."

Later that evening, after I return home, I think about Nancy's questions, "Why are you doing this now? Why would you do that to yourself?" And I have my answer:

> I want to read these letters now, when my feelings are raw and my heart is bleeding—not when everything is tempered by time, not when my emotions have subsided and reading them becomes simply an enjoyable experience. I want to read them when my eyes are blurred with tears and my heart is aching. I want to read them when the pain is so deep I can't imagine ever feeling anything other than this again. I want to feel Maggie with me, alive and here, not just as some fading memory.

***

I'm addicted to the letters. Every day I read them, they bring Maggie back, keep her by my side and make me realize what I had in my life. I only wish I would have been more aware, more keenly aware of this when Maggie was alive. I know we loved each other deeply and I know she knew how very much I loved her. But the letters—the letters show me, give me the Maggie that was. I wish I would have read them ten or fifteen years ago—read them with the same intensity, the same sense of discovery I have now. I don't know if that would have even been possible. Would I have had the same epiphany or would our day-to-day life have clouded these realizations?

Reading the letters every day for the past three months, reading and organizing them, remains an absolutely cherished experience. It's as if I'm discovering a new Maggie every time I read one.

This is the Maggie I lost in the many challenges we faced during our lives together.

The Maggie I let fade through the daily rituals of marriage and raising four children.

The Maggie I forgot.

This is the Maggie I may have never really known.

I cry. I laugh. I get angry. I feel grateful. I feel stupid. I feel wise. I feel lucky. I feel blessed that Maggie became my wife and that I have these beautiful, beautiful letters.

CHAPTER 2

MAIL CALL

Mary Brown begins writing to me in July of 1965, shortly after she completed her junior year in high school. I'm twenty-four and in my second month of Army Basic Training. Mary Brown means little to me, but getting mail in Boot Camp from anyone means everything.

***

Sergeant Rodriguez stands tall and rigid, silhouetted in the opening of the front door.

"MAIL CALL!" he shouts.

"Mail call!" echoes throughout the barracks. Soldiers hurl themselves from their bunks, decks of cards are left scattered across foot lockers, comic books are abandoned, partially shined boots are cast aside, and conversations end in mid-sentence. Ordered from exiting through the front, everyone races to the back of the barracks, squeezes through the opened door, scampers around the side, and comes to a jolting halt at the front steps. Soldiers pool at the bottom of the wooden stairs—a puddle of Army green. Sgt. Rodriquez stands on the top step with a stack of letters in his left hand.

The weather doesn't matter—blazing sun or pouring rain—the men stand patiently, gazing up anxiously at Sergeant Rodriquez, waiting for their names to be called, waiting for words from their loved ones, hoping at least one of the letters in the stack in Sgt. Rodriquez's left hand is for them.

***

Boot Camp is going to be pure misery and we know it the minute we step off the bus onto the red clay of Ft. Gordon. We no longer belong to the world we left—we belong to the Army. More precisely, we belong to Sgt. Rodriquez.

"YOU'RE MINE MEAT!" Sgt. Rodriquez bellows as we scramble off the bus and hastily form two rows abreast, stumbling and repeatedly bumping into each other until we become two haphazard lines facing the booming voice. He's the picture on the recruiting poster: tall and thin, but muscular and deeply tanned by the blazing Georgia sun. His Army fatigues are tailored tight, with his pants neatly tucked and slightly bloused over his spit-shined boots. His drill instructor's hat is tilted forward to hide his eyes, making him even more intimidating. He's the elite of the elite. As he slowly paces up and down the ragged lines hollering orders, he repeatedly swats his right thigh with a riding crop to show he's totally oblivious to pain.

"For the next two months, you're mine. You're gonna wish you were never in this man's Army, because you ain't men, you're pieces of meat—you're nothin' but meat and I'm the grinder. You're gonna wish you never met me."

And for the next two months, Sergeant Rodriquez couldn't have been more right. He did his damndest to make us feel like the pieces of meat he declared we were.

For the first month of Basic Training, there's little contact with the world outside Ft. Gordon. Ft. Gordon is our world now. We're awakened at 6 a.m. every day by a wooden bat slamming against the metal posts of our bunks and Sgt. Rodriguez's morning wakeup call "Get up! Get up! Up! Up! Up!!! Get your asses out of bed! Get up! Move it! Move it! GET UP!! GET UP!!" We scamper from our bunks, fumble to get into our fatigues and our boots, banging into our bunkmate or the guy in the bunk next to us, almost falling as we try to maintain our balance. Sgt. Rodriquez's booming voice constantly exhorts, "Move it! Move it! MOVE IT!" And we move it. We don't know where we're moving it to, but we move it and we move it damn fast because if we don't, we face the wrath of Sgt. Rodriquez. He can't hit us—it's against military regulations, but he can dress us down so badly in front of our platoon that we wish he would have hit us and saved us the embarrassment.

We march in the scalding sun across the melting red clay of Georgia. And we do push-ups in the sand during the pouring rain until we're so tired our arms buckle and our faces splatter in the puddle beneath us. We trudge up hills and run down hills until our legs are numb. And we cross swamps, chest high, with our rifle held above our head because our rifle is our "friend" and we aren't allowed to let our "friend" get wet; and if our "friend" does get wet, it sleeps in our bunk that night while we sleep on the floor. And we polish our boots every day, knowing we will be slogging through the mud the next morning and polishing our boots again that night. We clean the toilets with a fingernail brush and scrub the bathroom floor and showers with a washcloth. And we're told we love it because we're in "this man's Army" and we belong to Sgt. Rodriquez. And if he says "you love it," you had better love it.

***

Mail is our only link to the world that once was—our only link to those who love us, or who we hope at least care enough to see if we still exist. Mail proves there is a world out there—and maybe, just maybe, we're still part of it. Mail connects us to that world outside Ft. Gordon, outside our barracks, outside the piercing voice of Sgt. Rodriquez.

"Smith!"

"Here, Sergeant!"

"Evans!"

"Here, Sergeant!"

"Riley!"

"Here, Sergeant!"

Never in alphabetical order. Would it be so difficult to put the envelopes in alphabetical order? If they were, I could anticipate when my name might be called and slink away when Sgt. Rodriquez goes past it. I could sneak away before most of the other grunts know I didn't get anything. But because they're never in alphabetical order, I have to wait in the blazing sun or drenching rain until the name on the last envelope is read—just in case. And when that last letter isn't for me and I feel the pain of no one caring enough to write, I can't slink away anymore, because there are too few soldiers left to allow me to leave unnoticed. Just a few of us, heads down, boots kicking the red clay, moving back into the barracks, back to the abandoned comic books, or the half-shined boots, or the game of poker, because no one cared enough to let us know there's still a world outside Ft. Gordon.

Sometimes Sgt. Rodriquez mispronounces my name: "Deceptic!" or "Depicek!" At first, I think it's just an innocent mistake, but maybe it's not. And sometimes he's so far off I have no idea my name is being called.

"Delepoi!"

No answer.

"Private Delepoi!"

Silence, still.

When there's no response, Sgt. Rodriquez puts the letter at the back of the stack and proceeds with calling all the others, then goes back and repeats the name on the unclaimed letters, giving a little more information.

"Delepoi! Return address Bonfield Street, Chicago!"

"Oh, here Sergeant, that must be me."

"Then why didn't you answer the first time I called it! Get your head out of your ass, Private!"

My mother sends letters all the time, at least two a week. They never say much. Just that she hopes I'm doing well, or she's going to paint the kitchen, or our dog, Daisy, was sick last week. But they let me know someone out there remembers me and cares enough to write. I enjoy getting them, but it quickly becomes known that almost all my letters are from my mother, and letters from moms simply don't hold the same weight as letters from a girlfriend.

When I get my first letter from Mary Brown, my bunkmate, Stan, sarcastically questions me from above.

"Another letter from your mom, Depcik?"

"No. It's from a girl."

"Who?"

"Mary Brown."

"Yeah, sure, Depcik. Who's she, Jane Doe's sister?"

But it is from Mary Brown. And she sends several more when I'm in Boot Camp. I appreciate them because Mary Brown's a girl and she's not my mother. No one needs to know she's my sister-in-law's kid sister, only seventeen and has just completed her junior year in high school.

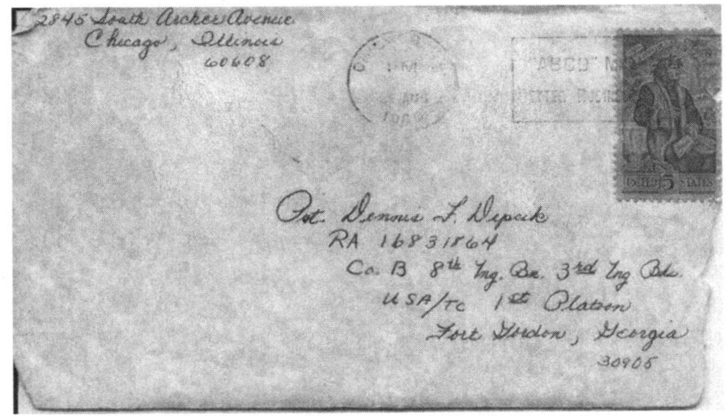

The few letters Mary Brown sends are amusing. I know from her sister that Mary's had a school-girl crush on me since we stood up at the wedding four years ago. I like the idea of getting mail from this "Maggie," as she prefers to be called, and I answer her when I have time. She's cute, but she's seven years younger than me, only a kid, a pleasant pen pal.

August 25, 1965

Dear Dennis, "Our Protectorate"

Hi and how goes it? I wasn't going to write this soon, but since your apologies were so sincere (Ha Ha), I decided to forget about the racks, ropes and any other punishments. Please don't apologize for not being able to answer all my letters. I don't want you to feel that you "owe" me an answer. I write to you because I enjoy it, silly.

So, they're breaking you away from marching. How do you expect to keep in shape? Speaking of shape, I'm on a crash diet! Did you ever have celery for breakfast? It doesn't work. Oh well, what's a couple of unwanted pounds here and there... and here and there...and here and there.... I always did want to go out for football!

If working with grenades, bazookas and 45 mil. caliber pistols isn't exciting! The closest I've ever come to that much excitement is when the air-raid siren goes off every Tuesday at 10:30 a.m. and our teachers make us crawl underneath our desks. Once they made us go in the basement and say the rosary, but that was way back before Superman died.

I haven't decided if I should go into a career or get married. Should I go out and earn a man's salary or stay home and take it away from him? I've heard of the gal who refused a man's marriage proposal and they both lived happily ever after. Actually, I think I have more of a maternal instinct and should just find a job till the right crackpot – I mean jackpot comes along. Do you realize after this speedy senior year, I'll be on my own? When I was a freshman, I couldn't wait and now I'm getting shaky! I really can't believe how the time flew by.

Well, patriotic soul, I better get my housework done before I turn into one of those women who sleep until noon and greet their husbands in a raggedy robe and a head full of curlers. So, until your next letter (Ahem), please take care and stay happy always.

As Mostly??
As Always,
Unsinkable Maggie

CHAPTER 3

PEN PALS AND POETS

The past year has been hectic, adventurous, challenging, and very, very lucky. I completed Basic and Advanced Infantry Training, as well as six months of intensive training at Infantry Officer Candidate School (OCS). Shortly after entering OCS, the conflict in Vietnam began to escalate. The increased involvement of U.S. combat troops necessitated a steady supply of infantry officers. I wasn't a gung-ho soldier when I joined the Army and didn't envision myself leading a platoon into combat. I simply wanted to meet my draft obligation, get my tour of duty over and get back to civilian life.

As luck or my mother's prayers would have it, in March of 1966, a month before graduating from OCS, I was notified that I would be transferred to the Armed Forces Courier Service—only one of two candidates receiving such a transfer. I was ecstatic and felt good fortune couldn't shine any brighter, but soon discovered it could. When my orders came, I learned I was assigned to courier duty in Chateauroux, France, and would be delivering classified material in Western Europe.

***

It's April 18, 1966, and I'm home on a two-week leave between graduating from OCS and leaving again for two months of courier training. My parents host a small dinner in my honor, nothing big, just a small family get-together and some good Polish food. My brother, Leo, and his wife, Patsy, who still live in the flat above my parents, join us and bring Maggie, who had stopped by to visit her sister. As usual, it's a quiet dinner with very little talking. My parents believe dinnertime is for eating, not talking. So, we sit in silence with only an occasional comment.

When dinner is over, we all move to the front room where I show slides I took while I was stationed in Georgia. Besides pictures of my OCS experience and some local sites, I have multiple slides of ducks: ducks swimming, ducks flying, ducks landing in a lake, ducks waddling across a street.

Finally, my father asks the obvious, "What's with all the ducks?"

I'm not sure why the ducks fascinated me, so I simply reply, "I don't know. I guess because they were there. Anyway, I'm thinking of starting a photo collection."

After I put away the slide projector and screen, I notice Maggie sitting alone in the corner of the couch, seeming a bit out of place, staring straight ahead. To be polite, I walk over. "Hey, Maggie, how's school going?"

Maggie jumps, startled by my unexpected nearness.

"Oh, I'm sorry. What'd you ask me?"

I sit next to her and for a few minutes we talk about the weather, the latest pop hits, and some of our immediate plans. Maggie mentions she's really excited about entering some nurses training program in Chicago after she graduates high school, and I share my excitement about going to Europe. We thank each other for our letters and Maggie apologizes for not writing in such a long time. There's been so much going on in my military life, I never realized she had stopped, but I tell her not to worry about it. Actually, until I saw her this evening, I barely thought about her.

***

After I completed courier training in early July of 1966, I was stationed in Chateauroux, France—145 miles south of Paris. I knew my stay there would be brief, since French President, Charles De Gaulle, had already ordered all American troops to get out. I didn't know where I'd be going when the Chateauroux station closed, but I assumed I'd remain somewhere in Europe, since the Army made this assignment knowing full well we'd be leaving France. But, then again, it *is* the Army and I've learned one thing in my short tour of duty—don't expect logical thinking.

Again, God's hand or Lady Luck tapped me on the shoulder. In early August I was not only transferred to Germany, but to the courier station at USAREUR Headquarters in beautiful Heidelberg.

Since my transfer, I've received a couple letters from my sister-in-law. In one, she casually mentions that Maggie graduated from high school and got engaged. I paid little attention to the news, except to think seventeen was awfully young for any girl to get engaged.

Mary (Maggie) Brown, engaged shortly after graduating high school.

I've been in Heidelberg a little over a month and I absolutely love Germany. In France, I seemed to be an intruder every place I went. Germany is so different—I actually feel welcome here. I would have expected it to be the other way around.

I still can't believe my good fortune. Friends of mine are fighting in the rice paddies and jungles of Vietnam and somehow I get this assignment. It doesn't seem right, but I'm not going to tempt fate by questioning it. Because of the situation in France, I haven't been on many courier trips. I'm really excited about traveling to cities like Munich, Rome, Brussels, and Berlin—all the places I read about in my history books. Imagine me, a blue-collar kid from Bridgeport in Chicago, traveling to places I'd only heard of—Lieutenant Depcik, Mr. Cosmopolitan.

Well, Mr. Cosmopolitan is homesick. As excited as I am about my future adventures, I miss my family, my friends, and anything that's part of my world that was. I look forward to a letter from home as much as any new courier assignment. I still long to hear from my family and about what's happening in the neighborhood, because any news keeps me connected to those I love.

Every workday morning near lunch time, Cpl. Russell picks up the mail from the base post office and distributes it to all of us in the station. As I shuffle through the few pieces he hands me today, I find a letter from my mother and one from Maggie Brown. The last time my mother wrote, she mentioned she wasn't feeling well, and I'm anxious to see if everything's okay. After reading her letter, I'm relieved to learn all the family news: she's "back to her old self," my sister has a new boyfriend, and our dog, Daisy, got into another fight with our neighbor's cat—and lost again.

Content in my knowledge that all is well at home, I pick up Maggie Brown's letter. I can't remember the last time she wrote, but I recognize her return address and her handwriting. How did she know I was transferred to Heidelberg? Her sister must have given her my new address.

September 6, 1966

Dear Dennis,

Please don't feel committed to answer this letter as it is just to let you know that the "Beauty of Bridgeport" is still alive and thinking of you. (Nothing personal, of course).

So, are there any ducks where you're stationed? Whatever you do, get their pictures! It'll add something to that collection that you already have. And besides, I enjoy Ooohing and Ahhing at duck pictures.

I've heard so many great things about Germany. I know the people are supposed to idolize American soldiers and the scenery is really fantastic. Anyway, I do hope it has a lot to offer you and that your stay will be a pleasant experience. I do expect you to get a little work done though.

Just two more weeks and I'll begin training at St. Vincent's. I'm really a little nervous about the whole ordeal as I don't know what to expect. I can't wait to get started though.

Bob is still at Ft. Sill, Oklahoma. He just made PFC two weeks ago, but is now waiting for orders which may or may not send him to Viet Nam. He won't know until a month or so, so the pressure hasn't quite hit him yet.

Well, I guess I've taken up enough of your time. Please take care and try to write.

As Always
Maggie

It's nice to hear from Maggie again. She still has that subtle sense of humor I remember from her previous letters. I like that. I think I'll have some fun with her.

Around 13 September 1966

Dear Beauty:

How absurd of you to tell me you are alive. I am not a complete illiterate you know. I do read the papers. Certainly the death of such a renowned individual as yourself would have made the headlines of every international paper - even the "Stars and Stripes" which last week newsworthily (if there is such an adverb) exclaimed in bold print that Colonel Bassface's guppies had the measles.

God, I'm going crazy. I've combed this country from top to bottom and I can't find any ducks. What in the world will become of my budding collection? Maybe I have a solution. On the flight over, I took numerous pictures of cloud formations. Now, there ain't no place in this world I can go that ain't got no clouds. I've been told that every intelligent person has a hoby and I deafinitlee want to be non as an intelligent.

I wrote a poem. Tell me if you understand it:

Today I am
What one day I wasn't
And tomorrow I'll be
Another me.

A stream briskly flows
And takes inside
All that will enter
Then casts aside
What it can't contain
And carries the rest
That still remains
Til it crashes the rocks
With such a sound
That warns the world
It won't be bound.

I'm not a pool
That stagnant and deep
Receives the new
And refuses to keep
It hidden within
But belches it up
When stirred by the wind.

Always Me,
Dennis

P.S. I addressed the letter as I did to impress the postman.

Early October 1966

Dear Dennis, fellow intellectual,

Would you believe I'm not sure that I understand your poem? I know you meant it for yourself, but I couldn't help applying it to myself. Now I'm very depressed and very confused. The lines...

that warns the world
it won't be bound

These lines are my favorite and the cause of all my confusion. Maybe I'm not the intellectual that I thought I was, (ha ha) or perhaps I'm too much me, (not poundage wise either), but I don't want to be another me. Is that wrong? Dennis!!!

Here's my poem. Prepare yourself for a good hardy-har. I write such baby poetry.

Even when I talk of love
my fear is open for review
And when I talk of hate
my eagerness to hate shows through

I try to hide the thoughts I think
I try to make them go away
but nasties prompt me with a wink
and naked thoughts come out to play

(SEX) Now that I have your attention once again, would you like to know my latest hobby? No? Well anyway, I've started a paper-back library/ intellectual??? Really, I'm becoming a fiend as far as books are concerned. I have about thirty books right now, but only twenty are worthwhile. I know I should broaden my view and collect biographies, poetry, etc., but I have this "thing" about novels. I guess I should call it simply a novel library. Cute???

My voice is in very good oohing and ahhing condition, since I practice these exclamatory (if there is such an adjective) sounds each time I look in the mirror. Sorry to say that it isn't very often, though.

My eyes can take it, but the mirror can't. (Hey, there is such an adjective).

By the time you get this, I'll be in school. My feelings towards it are tearing me apart. I'm filled with anxiety to begin training, and yet I lack the confidence to give the course the all-out American one...two....

Well, Dennis, I guess I'll end this before you think that I'm completely out of my mind. Good luck on your next adventure. Keep your eyes and your spirits on those cloud formations, but remember to keep your head down to earth.

As Always,
me...Maggie
(Beauty???)

P.S. Hey! Beauty was a horse!!! Well!
P.S.S. Write soon (if you dare)

Mid October 1966

My Dear Miss Magathie:

Did you answer my last letter? If not, my heart stands broken and bleeding. If you did, it may have already been returned to you because my address has changed.

I wrote a couple more poems since my last letter. No lesson to learn here, no profound ideas (if any of my ideas have ever been profound), simply an honest attempt to create a certain mood:

Silent ship, upon a silent sea,
Under a setting sun
Pushed by a gentle breeze
Which whispers to the sails
And puffs their airy pride
To cross the sea, soundlessly
And gain the other side.

and:

A leaf which cannot last
The lure of Autumn's song
Dances through the air
And lights within a pool.

The startled host awakened
By this unexpected visit
Softly taps the hand
Of the sleeping land.

Leaf, land and pool
In solemn silence sit,
Hushed audience –
Mute in reverence.

Patiently Waiting,
Dennis

Of the letters discovered in the Neiman Marcus box, there are none from me to Maggie from mid-October 1966 to mid-July 1967—nine months. I know I wrote letters because Maggie refers to them in hers, but I don't know why they're not among those saved.

I had continued to save Maggie's letters.

CHAPTER 4

A FLICKER OF LOVE

October 21, 1966

Dear Dennis,

Please, no bloodshed, but I do owe you two letters. Honestly, it wasn't that I hadn't thought about you, but I just had no time or perhaps no energy.

Yes, I'm a pretty busy character now that I'm a Student Nurse. My hours are really confusing, but I love what I'm doing. I've never felt so complete in all my life. I know I still have a long way to go before I'm really a person though.

Den, you're really something to figure out. How can a duck-lover like you sit down and write such beauty in a few little poems? I really mean that.

Hey! I hear you're working for a priest! That's pretty good for a guy living in the beer villa of the world. Do you enjoy using your spare time in this way? I would think that you'd be out stealing the hearts of all the fair maidens that flock around you as you step from your doorway.

You know, I miss you. Bridgeport, especially Bonfield street, just isn't the same anymore. Everything is so ho-hum! And what will Christmas be like without one of your serenades?

I wish you would let me in on more of what you're doing. I guess people as important as you can't afford to waste time writing long letters. Anyway, just hearing from you is just as great as if you had written a whole encyclical to me.

Well, Den, I have to get ready for work. Please accept my apology if you find this letter too lengthy or too boring. Remember to take care and as always, stay happy.

Missing you,
Magathie

P.S. Write soon

Well, how about that. She signed her name "Magathie." This kid really does have a sense of humor. That's going to be my name for her from now on, "Miss Magathie."

October 31, 1966

Dear Dennis,

Please don't ever think that I feel obligated to write to you. I'm just so glad that you want my letters. It really is all my pleasure.

Den, I really have to look up to you. You really are "living." What other man in your situation would devote his time teaching catechism. In my last year of high school we went over the "hot" subjects of our modern world and never came to any conclusions. My ideas were <u>*unaltered*</u> *and I still can't focus my confusion. Someday, if you ever have time, I wish you'd help me figure out some problems and questions that I have about 20th Century Christian living.*

Who's flattering who? You make me sound like Joan of Arc! Oh, Den, I do love the babies at St. Vincent's. You don't know how I feel to be called "Mommy" (they associate "white" with mommy). They look at you with such empty eyes. I'm afraid that if I look at them they'll see too much compassion and sometimes down right pity. I don't want to pity them, so I try loving them. It works, Den. They are so love-starved and yet so full of love.

Do you think I'm a lot like my sister? I don't!! I admit in some respects we are definitely similar, but please don't classify me as "just like her sister, Patsy." You'd be surprised to know how different we really are.

Yes, I do miss you. It may seem silly since I never really knew you and am just learning to know you now. Somehow I feel closer to you now.

Hey, I wasn't being sarcastic about your singing. However, I do prefer when you just move your lips (only kidding).

Well, Den, I guess it's about time to polish my white shoes and perhaps hit a book or two.

Please don't forget to write soon and remember to stay happy.

Sincerely,
Magathie

P.S. Be careful in that Black Forest! You lucky---
I'd give anything to go on a sleigh ride - just once.

November 10, 1966

Dear Dennis,

Thank you again for sending me your poems. They really are lovely and I enjoy them so much. Honestly, I'm not trying to flatter you.

How are your catechism classes coming along? In my religion course, I have to see my teacher after class tomorrow. I answered a question honestly and have now found myself in a mix-up. The question was - "If a child has not learned to trust in earlier years, will he find it difficult to do so in adolescence or adulthood?" I answered to the effect that as I myself am growing older I find it more difficult to have faith in people. Maybe I'm a little mixed up because of my dad and all, but I can honestly say that there is only one person (my girlfriend, Cathy) who I can place an absolute trust in. Is there something wrong with me? I'm not saying I have no trust in people whatsoever, but I do feel absolute trust in people is limited.

Oh Den, I didn't mean to sound snappy or accuse you of labeling me as "just like her sister, Patsy." We may have the same, you know I can't think of one way that we're the same. I can't get over how different we really are. Even our needs are different! I must agree we both love nursing, but she looks upon it as a way of learning and experiencing where I look at it as a way of loving and needing. I can't really explain it. You probably think I'm out of my mind or perhaps entirely wrong, but I know my sister and I'm just beginning to know myself. I've always thought I had to be just like her. It's so silly! I strove to be May Queen, because she was May Queen. I studied hard to keep par with her grades, I tried so hard to be a carbon copy...and I almost did it until I found out I wasn't. That's why I jumped on you for comparing me to Patsy. I've heard that all my life and if people could only discover that I'm

Maggathie and not "just as good as Patsy." Thank you for discovering it.

Dennis, I really am sorry if I bent your ear – I mean your eyes!!? I will let you go now, so here's to your sigh of relief.

As Always,
Maggathie

P.S. Write soon

P.S.S. You didn't sign your last letter. Thank goodness for return addresses and unique handwriting, although the style of your letter writing speaks for your signature!

The conflict in Vietnam continues to escalate and the flow of classified material through the Heidelberg Courier Station is increasing considerably. We're making far more frequent trips to allied European countries and I have very limited time to write letters to anyone. But at least I can send Christmas cards to my parents and a couple friends.

Maggie didn't receive my Christmas card until after she sends the following letter.

December 20, 1966

Dear Dennis,

Dear? What did you do, break an arm? Thanks for sending me a Christmas card, pal.

How is everything going? I hope you're keeping active and free from the state of boredom.

I certainly could go for some leisure time. My crazy hours at the hospital keep me going all the time. I haven't had the chance to do so much as watch a simple T.V. show. Well, maybe one.

I'm just getting rid of a depressed feeling. In fact, I nearly gave up a few days ago. I seriously thought of quitting, but as much as I hate the hours and pay, something gets into your blood when you've been there for awhile.

I put up my skimpy Christmas tree and is it ever bad news. It's one of the first silver trees that came out with a whole 25 crushed branches. When you look at it, you get the feeling that it doesn't like you, but somehow it puts a little Christmas spirit in the house.

My dad is moving out February 3rd. He's retiring. It isn't as bad as it sounds. He'll probably still find time to come around now and then.

I was elected President of the Student Council at school. I was really shocked as commuters rarely make officers because of the crazy hours that meetings are held. I live at school more than at home though, so it won't make too much difference.

Oh, I painted my kitchen again and well --- did you ever hear about hit and miss?

Well, dear heart, I won't ask you to write as I wouldn't want you to strain yourself, but if you ever get the inspiration, please do.

As Always,
Magathie
Oops forgot
2 g's
Sorry about that

P.S. Are you conceited?
P.S.S. Please excuse the classy paper, but .... I can't think of an excuse

Maggie sounds a little upset. I wonder why? It's not unusual for me to go several weeks without writing and it usually doesn't bother her. This time it's different.

A simple Christmas card from Maggie with a return address from her nurses training program.

December 23, 1966

Dear Dennis

Please accept my apology for accusing you of forgetting me this Christmas.

I really wish you were here even if only to blast the neighborhood with a chorus of Jingle Bells (you could always carry along a radio and just move your lips).

I hope you get this in time, but what is more important is that you have a blessed Christmas and that your every dream for the coming year come true.

Sincerely,
Maggathie

I unexpectedly come home Christmas morning. It's pure luck that I have to deliver some classified material to Washington D. C. on Christmas Eve and am able to add a couple days to travel to Chicago. Because I was home for a short leave in April and am now stationed in Heidelberg, no one expects me home again this soon; the tears in my mother's eyes when she answers my knock on the door makes all the harried airport arrangements and lost sleep insignificant. From that merry moment, Christmas day couldn't be more enjoyable.

The following evening, my parents invite my brother and his wife to have dinner with us. Since Maggie was invited to her sister's for dinner because her father was out of town, my mother has no problem including her. Leo asks if I can do him a favor and pick Maggie up from the nurses training program at St. Vincent's Orphanage and Infant Hospital and bring her to the house.

On the near north side of Chicago, St. Vincent's is only a twenty-minute drive from my parents' home. It's an old, massive, brown stone building spread over a half block, with four large pillars holding a brick canopy as you enter the main lobby.

A receptionist dressed in white sits behind the front desk. As I approach, I can see she's busy filling out paperwork, her eyes rigidly cast down. I walk to the front of the desk and stand quietly for a few seconds, assuming she will acknowledge my being there. Engrossed in paperwork or indifferent to my presence, her head doesn't budge.

"Excuse me," I whisper.

She doesn't move.

"Excuse me!" I whisper a little louder. "I don't mean to intrude."

She abruptly places her pencil to the side of her papers, slowly lifts her head, looks askance at me and in an annoyed voice says, "Yes! Can I help you?"

"I'm here to pick up Mary Brown."

"Is she expecting you?"

"I'm pretty sure she is. I'm supposed to give her a lift home."

Without even asking my name, she sighs in exasperation, runs her fingers down a list on the right side of her desk, reaches for the phone on her left, and dials three numbers. A few seconds pass. Then, in a patronizing voice, she says, "Would you tell Mary Brown her ride is here."

She abruptly places the phone on its cradle, turns slowly to me and coldly says, "Mary Brown will be down shortly." Then, as if pulled by a giant magnet, her head is immediately drawn back to her paperwork.

I'm not sure what I should do next. Does she want me to stand here and wait? I look around for a place to sit and see two wooden benches against the wall about fifteen feet behind me. There are no magazines and I always feel awkward sitting in an empty room with nothing to read. I never know where to put my hands or whether or not I should cross my legs. So I stand there, hands behind my back, with nothing to do but stare at the ceiling, count the tiles on the floor, and wonder how long "shortly" will be. The receptionist keeps her head riveted to her paperwork and is once again oblivious to my presence.

Within ten minutes, the "Mary Brown who will be down shortly" walks through the double doors that lead from the interior of the orphanage. I don't know what I was expecting, but I'm surprised to see her dressed in a white nurse's uniform, white stockings, white shoes, looking—different.

When she sees me, she stops immediately. Her mouth opens slightly, her eyes widen, and she stutters, "Oh—oh my God, it's you—I didn't know you were home—I was expecting Leo—this is really a surprise—when did you get home—I didn't expect to see you—I mean—it's nice to see you—Hi."

I can't help but smile and be somewhat flattered by her awkwardness in my presence.

"Leo asked if I would pick you up. Hope you don't mind. I'm only home for a couple days."

We stand motionless for a few seconds—Maggie's hands clasped in front, mine cupped behind my back—just looking at each other and both feeling a little uncomfortable.

The lady in white at the front desk lifts her head slowly toward us and watches our little drama unfold before quickly returning to the all-consuming paperwork.

Maggie breaks the tense silence. "Just let me get my purse."

As she goes to push open the double doors that lead to the orphanage, she stops and turns to me. "Would you like to see the orphanage? It won't take long."

"Sure." And I quickly follow her through the opened doors.

Maggie takes me through several wards, introducing me to the nurses and fellow students as "Dennis, my brother-in-law's brother, who's home from the Army for Christmas." As we walk through the wards, Maggie points out her favorite babies, giving a brief history of each. Whenever she picks up a baby, she cradles it gently in her arms close to her chest, hugs it against her cheek for several seconds, and speaks in hushed tones before gently placing it back in the crib. Whenever she holds a baby, her eyes gleam, her smile widens, and her voice softens. There's a glow about her. *Is this my sister-in-law's kid sister? Is this the bumbling kid I just saw in the waiting room?* I'm mesmerized by the transformation.

During the course of the tour, we lose track of time and the fact that forty-five minutes have passed. Realizing this, we hurriedly walk through the remaining wards and quickly depart. In the short drive to my parents' house, we briefly talk about the nurses program, Maggie's fiancé, and a few of my trips in Europe. Upon arriving, everyone is waiting; dinner is ready and some family members are not too happy about our late entrance. But it's Christmastime; I'm home for only two days; and soon the cold stares turn to holiday smiles.

After dinner, I show slides of sights I saw in Europe. I'm fortunate to have traveled to several countries and have slides of not only Germany, but Paris, Brussels, and Amsterdam. When I finish, my brother quips, "What, no ducks?" We later sing Christmas carols as Maggie and her sister take turns playing the piano.

All through the evening, I can't stop sneaking peeks at Maggie. She doesn't seem to be the kid I always thought she was. There's something about her, and I don't know what. I'm in a state of confused wonderment.

When the night ends, I offer to walk Maggie home, since she lives only a block away. It's a bitter cold night, but we walk slower than the weather should allow. During that fifteen-minute walk, Maggie and I talk about the weather, Barbra Streisand, our preference of chocolate or vanilla ice cream, who wrote to whom last, and other such momentous topics. When we reach the front door to Maggie's building, I offer to walk her up the two flights to her apartment. Maggie politely says it isn't necessary, and that I "have already done enough." As I begin to open the entrance door, pushing it aside so Maggie can pass, I have this urge to kiss her, hesitate, then let my better judgment rule over impulse and simply say, "Good night, Maggie. I had a good time."

Maggie turns, looks up at me, pauses for a few seconds, and says, "So did I. Thanks for bringing me home."

I walk away as she slowly closes the door.

For the next thirteen months, Maggie and I neither see nor speak to each other. Our only communication is through our letters.

December 27, 1966

Dear Dennis,

Well, handy Andy, I decided to write to you first seeing that I (ahem) owe you a letter. I hope you had a pleasant trip although as I write this you are still in flight.

Will you do me a favor? Next time, take snapshots. Actually, I had a wonderful time last night. Thank you for making it wonderful. And don't write saying it was your pleasure - you always say that when you do things for me. Gallant?

You know, I miss you. Now, isn't that silly. I've been in the same room with you about 5 times in the last year, I've driven with you twice, you came home for 48 hours out of which approximately 6 hours were spent anywhere near me, and I miss you! All I need is a question mark over my head.

I wrote a poem --- Stop laughing, Dennis! Of course it will never compare to your poetic works (and I mean that) but at least I gave it the old Maggathie try! I'm sending it anyway, smarty. Will you stop laughing!!

Here it is
Hey, play some violin music - it needs something

> *When a doll dies*
> *Only a child knows the pain*
> *of the forever putting away into the attic*
> *the laughing days a doll brought.*
>
> *When ponies can't romp*
> *through quilt meadows of dreams*
> *because they're lost*
> *on the dime-store smell threshold of cities*
> *only a child knows the silence of vacant saddles.*

When a clown falls mouth wracked
to the floors of circus dust
only a child dies and bends her
empty bosom to the fallen heart.

When a child fails
to breathe the breath of laughter
only a bird
wings lifeless through sullen trees.

THE END

No #2

Deep in the emotions of loneliness
Silent tears and an empty heart
  are put away so others can't see

Unsmiling silver eyes and chapped knuckles
  don't seem to care what has happened
  but wait for something

I'm young and alone
and throughout dark days
I am learning to live with myself.
I've picked up again and as I look
  at the clock I thank the
    city for trying
  but hope for his coming.

THE END

Well, I goofed that second part up, but the gist of it is still there. I think. Sorry about that.

Well, Dennis, I better go get my beauty sleep---I need it. Please write to me.

Do you actually mean I won't be hearing that masculine voice again for another year and a half? Oh Dennis, that will never do. Couldn't you make a record or something?

Love,
Maggathie XXIII

P.S. Don't forget to write.

January 5, 1967

My Dear Denny? Denny?

My Dear Denny, --- I mean Dennis

Hi! I nearly flipped to find a letter from you today as I am honored that you find time to write to plain old Maggathie. I'm not a flatterer as I only write what I feel and my feelings are sincere. So, Den, you still remain the master flatterer.

Why should you want to extract your ball point simply because you haven't anything exciting to say? If it weren't for your letters, I'd be lost for words. You always seem to either ruffle my feathers or make my heart flutter so that I have something to comment on. If I used exciting news as guidelines for writing, I'd have to depend on my memorial experiences such as my First Holy Communion in 1955 or the day my finger got caught in the opening of a Hershey syrup can in 1960.

I really do miss you. I thought it over and found about fifteen to twenty reasons for my feelings, but I won't tell you as you'd probably only laugh.

You honestly want me to send you another poem? Isn't that great! Dennis, a college graduate, wanting to read one of my nicketty scrabbles of thought. I have three poems which you haven't seen yet. I wrote them within the last three months and they all seem to deal with the same subject. So, I'll only send you two, the two which are the least alike.

Your last poem made me feel a little guilty about writing (or I should say) trying to write poetry:

"stuffed and stretched into a truth
the author hardly knows."

How true that is. Oh that was the part that I marveled at.

Well, here I go again –

The clear wind comes crying...
pressing its time-weathered lips
against mine...
playing some soul's song to the sea,
beach grasses bowed
and sand traveled with no luggage.

You called from behind the hill
walking back I thought
This shall be a memory, a secret
for the Sea, wind and me.

There are so many poems about the sea and everything, but I wrote this during the summer. You see, I'm always daydreaming and it seems I'm always being interrupted without anyone actually questioning my thoughts. So, that was my inspiration and you'll have to figure things out from there. THERE!

This is just too much for me, but you asked for it

You have turned on the warm faucet
of memory
lodged deep and long
It all comes bubbling out now
Rusty and not quite clear
saturating my mind
with foggy happenings,
damp vows,
And tangled dreams that could never
be unwound.

Gazing in the mirror
my reflection blurred
from precipitation on the glass
and in my eyes.

I wish you'd leave
So I could remember you
with the scent of green timber
before it's aged.

Oh well -- I tried ---

Now that that's over with. Den, -- WAKE UP, DEN!! Yoo Hoo!!

Den, I love writing to you but if I use any more of this paper I'll have about 10 pieces of it left and about 30 envelopes to dispose of. (Actually, you can always use envelopes)

Please try to write soon

Sincerely,
Maggathie

P.S. Don't be conceited. I like you better the way I know you.

Den, I'm sorry to bother you, but there's a question that I want to ask you. Something came up in the last few days and it's bothered me very much. I'm very worried about this. Do I give you the impression that the world owes me something? Someone brought this to my attention and I wondered if maybe it was true or not.

You don't know how bad I feel. I want you to answer in all honesty because if I do, I'll have some soul searching to do.

Thank you even if you may not be able to help.

Maggathie

January 28, 1967

Dear ?,

I don't know what to call you. Should I call you D, D^2, the Dep, the Big D, or Debbie. What in the world is wrong with ---

Dear Dennis,

I am no longer worried about other people's misinterpretations. I shall fumble along and do my best from now on. Now if I could determine where I'm fumbling to and if my best was better than it is, I might be able to get somewhere in this world. I may not be a rose, that's a rose, that's a rose, but I am a Mary Margaret, that's a Maggie, that's a Maggathie.

I have some news for you. Due to a financial situation that is beyond my control, I had to leave my babies at St Vincent's. My dad is retiring and I don't wish to be the millstone around his neck. I'm not trying to sound like I'm pitying myself, because I'm not. I owe so much to my father, that I could never think of standing in the way of his happiness.

I'm now an office "beauty" with little uniqueness and not much more of a display of accomplishments. I must say it feels good to be on my own. My fear is that I may be marked as a "quitter." I miss the hospital routine and most of all the babies, but then again, I'll have my own brew someday.

Thank you for the compliments on my rather unique phrases, but whatja 'spect' from a Bridgeportonian --"how now, brown cow"?

Your poems are really fabulous. I mean that. I detect a resentment toward marriage in the first one. They are expressive. I mean they must have taken a lot of thought. Oh, you know what I mean!!! (I think).

Please keep writing and take care always.

Love ya,
Maggathie

P.S. Sorry about the "Sincerelys." I didn't mean to get personal.

P.P.S. How do I know you? I know you as:
the gentleman who isn't a prude-
the intellectual who isn't a snob-
the fun-loving guy who isn't silly-
the advisor who isn't a gossip-
the handsome hunk of a man who isn't
conceited......

P.P.P.S. Please excuse my typing errors and any misuse of grammar. Whataya 'spect from a Bridgeportonian?

P.P.P.P.S. What did you mean when you said, quote: "What's with the 'Sincerely' stuff?"

CHAPTER 5

"WELL, I'M FREE NOW..."

Mid February 1967

Dear Dennis,

Your last letter made me the happiest I've been in a long time. You made me feel as if I were the most important person in the world to you and that alone is a feeling beyond compare. Warning: don't say things simply to uplift my spirit as they are immediately drawn to and absorbed by my heart.

What a relief to learn that you felt "Sincerely" was too impersonal. I have a confession to make. I meant sincerely with such intensity that I thought you would think it just the opposite of impersonal. I'm confused. Perhaps you don't read between the lines in my letters or maybe I read things in your letters that aren't actually written.

I do feel a special "something" toward you. It's not just my loneliness that causes this, as I have friends a plenty, but they're just not you. I can't explain what it is. For example I didn't actually care what others thought upon my leaving nursing, but I worried about how you'd feel. You're the last person I'd want to disappoint. I think the world of you, Dennis, and confidently, sometimes even more than that.

At this moment, I am very torn between telling you of all that I feel and the fear of saying too much. I'm glad I can at least be a little more at ease as I write. As much as I enjoy sharing your different experiences, I'm even more curious to learn of how you feel – your problems, hopes, fears etc. I just want to know all about you. It's funny, I do feel as if I know you, but I know too that there is much more that I must and want to learn.

Your Question

"What do you think I do, read your letters with a dictionary and grammar book by my side?"

My Answer

No, I think you have all that knowledge stored in that brain of yours.

In appreciation

Thank you for signing this latest letter. If you hadn't (and you usually don't) it would have ruined the whole thing.

Please excuse the coffee dribbles on the right side of this page.

A quote out of context from your last letter:

"... that I save your letters and often re-read them with increased pleasure and added admiration."

This is when my heart floated away. I lost my breath, my knees buckled and I knew I wasn't the same anymore.

In Admiration:

Thank you for trying to understand me.

"Helium phrases"? That's the closest anyone ever came to telling me I was full of hot air.

Dennis, if you wanted I'd have my portrait painted for you. I distinctly remember sending a picture -- check your miscellaneous file.

Love Ya!
Maggathie

Why is Maggie writing that she's *"...very torn between telling you all that I feel and the fear of saying too much"*? I'm definitely flattered, but I know she's engaged. I'm not sure where this is heading. I have to be careful.

Maggie's apartment on Archer Ave. where, at 18, she lives alone on the third floor after her father moves to Wisconsin. Her grandmother lives on the second floor, above the storefront.

February 24, 1967

Dear Dennis,

I can think of a dozen things I should be doing right now, but when that letter writing mood hits me, I become a fiend and you, my dear, are my victim.

I'm off today (Fri). My boss is out of town. I'll let you in on a secret. No matter what kind of a job I'll ever have, I'll never be happy. I could clean house and put up with kids for a lifetime, but that dog-eat-dog, pay-day, rush hour world just isn't for me. The closest I ever came to happiness was at St. Vincent's and I know now I'll never go back.

To boost my morale, I'm fixing up the house and making it a bachelorette flat. I've already started with essentials. I bought a new coffee pot and it's so nice to wake up to a cup of coffee without it meeting you half way. I bought a Teflon frying pan (how's that for class). The old pan was so warped it slid off the burner.

I'm saving for royal-blue, kelly-green tweed rugs. Don't worry; I won't hang a rope from the ceiling so people will glide across the room without walking on the precious things. I'm also getting this crazy white couch which has wild flowers all over and big fluffy pillows. When you look at it, it seems as if it was in the family for years.

This weekend I'm taking charge of my brother's four kids as he and his wife are going on a skiing trip in Wisconsin. To top that off, they're bringing a blind date home for me on Sunday. If I know my luck, he'll either be someone's obese brother or Baby Huey's twin. I am excited though. This will be my first date since I called off my engagement.

I'm beginning to worry about you. You haven't written in two weeks. Perhaps my last letter scared you off. Please don't feel that way. I may be very fond of you, but I'm not a "clinging vine."

I wrote a poem that probably won't make sense to you but---

I'm a child of yesterday's race
with quiet thoughts, modest pace.
I am one of soundless words
forever listening, but still often heard.
I dress myself in pink or blue
expressing myself as a child, true
I smile at thoughts of a cluttered mind
looking to things I'll never find
But through the years I will remain
the hope of future's sad refrain.

Please write soon

Love,
Maggathie

Did I just read that right—"*...my first date since I called off my engagement*"? How long ago did Maggie break her engagement? Why did she mention this so casually?

Late February 1967

Dear Dennis,

I must have at least three letters half written to you. Now at least I can start and finish this one.

Please don't be afraid to tell me the truth as I am not afraid to hear it. In my book, honest and sincere people are a rarity. You, Den, are one of the few who I can trust.

Your fear did not surprise me too much. For one thing, I knew it would have something to do with another's feelings. Also, I knew that you have been pursued by many enchanted young ladies, who, in turn, had not enchanted you. My only advice to you is that (and you've probably realized this since before I was even your brother's sister-in-law) when true love comes, you'll know her faults and accept them.

My fear is me. I'm either a mixed up character or I have a split personality. One day I'm declaring independence and the next day I'm needing someone to lean on. One minute I'm so happy-go-lucky and then the least little thing can make me feel as if the whole world was closing in on me. Sometimes I'm filled with a fiery passion and sometimes I want to be treated like a new born baby. When I find someone to understand that and put up with it, then I'll find "him." He'll have to be some great guy to be able to handle my enigmatic personality.

Wouldn't it be something if someday (2 centuries from now) someone discovered our letters to each other and wrote a novel about us? Maybe even an opera. Would you believe a science fiction movie?????

Did I tell you how my blind date turned out two weeks ago? The rat showed up at my brother's with a hangover. How about that! He looked like the type that could sell hotdogs on Maxwell Street. EIK!!!

Well, I better let you go before I start talking about the weather. One thing I can say is that we've been having a lot of it lately.

Please write soon as I can't wait to hear from you again. Even if you have to talk about the weather, write, write, write.

March 9, 1967

Dear Dennis,

Before I say one thing, I want you to know how proud I am that you, with the little time you have, can find the spare moments to write to me. You can't imagine how thrilled I am when I find a letter addressed to Miss Maggathie Brown.

Please don't be confused over me. I hope that the following explanation will straighten some matters out.

When I wrote that poem, I was trying to say that I would <u>*not*</u> *be perplexed by the anxiety of the future, but would remain rather composed. Whether I don't write what I feel, or don't feel what I write is the mystery. Perhaps my future poems should deal with the third person so that I can write what I write, and feel what I feel. No, poetry is supposed to deal with one's feelings. Well, back to the drawing board! At any rate, I would never be satisfied with the world if it were to remain as it was "in the good old days."*

I informed you of my broken engagement in such a manner so as to avoid sounding as if I were advertising it--- or as if to say, "Well, I'm free now, what are you gonna do about it?" I also believe that this change will not affect our relationship. I realize I am someone special to you, but hopes of becoming more than that are too far out of reach.

Well, I must go and do my weekly grocery shopping. You can't imagine the challenge I have living alone and on my own. I found out that I can't hammer a nail, can't budget, can't move furniture, can't paint very well, and can't have courage when I hear funny noises at night. Let's face it, "It's so nice to have a man around the house."

Please take care, and write soon, or as soon as time permits.

Love,
Maggathie

That Maggie is no longer engaged elates me. Who is this "Maggie," this kid, this sister-in-law's kid sister who likes to read my poems and writes her own; this Maggie who makes me smile when I read her letters—a smile that stays with me long after I return the letter to its envelope? Who is this Maggie who has a wisdom beyond her age; this Maggie who brightens my spirits and moves me in such a way that I yearn for her letters?

Yet, that she is no longer engaged frightens me. I don't know what my feelings are for her. I need to be careful. I might simply be reacting to Maggie's flattery. I may be missing the feeling of someone caring for me—someone who sees me as special. If this is all it is, I shouldn't lead her on—shouldn't let her think there's a possibility something can get started between us. I don't want this to go further than where I feel comfortable. I don't want Maggie falling for me when I'm not sure what I'm feeling for her.

CHAPTER 6

GETTING TO KNOW YOU

March 27, 1967

Dear Dennis,

Yes, hope is a wonderful virtue along with patience, understanding, knowledge, fortitude, and cleanliness of heart.

I am fortunate that I know a very cautious and somewhat subdued individual in you. I'm afraid that that old saying about learning about people through their letters is not always valid. It is true that I have come to know you better via air mail, but that's only because there is no other way. If we were ever to be alone together for more than ½ an hour, you would probably find yourself bored with my pleasant personality, or out of your mind trying to make sense out of what I say. For example, I bubble at the sight of something as common as a Christmas tree lit up in front of the Civic Center, and then again when the right time comes for words, I may freeze up! I'm just plain loopy....

I'm not talking about the weather now because I haven't anything else to say, but anyway...there's a sort of a spring here, although the sky hangs thick and once in a great while a ray of sun crashes through and melts in a puddle. You'd hardly know it, but there's a sort of spring here.

As for the thought of the day---It worries me to think that the foundation on which our Church is built could possibly fall apart by a few changes that have been delayed for so long. It will not affect my belief in the least if they were to rid of all that silly nonsense that has just been a glamorous trimming around the Truth. I always thought that some of our Church's "customs" were outdated and I felt rather guilty for thinking of them as such. Now I can trust in God without worrying about impressing Him with a false heart.

Your poem indeed deserved a comment, but I did not think that my silence would crush you. I think that you have a mind capable of beautiful thoughts, but one thing disturbs me and I must ask---------do you feel what you write or write what you feel? I'm not saying that your poems seemed to be lacking feeling, but that's a question that is still unsettled in my mind.

The first page of your last letter did not ring with conceit. It rang with mystery, and that's much better than conceit. I'm not quite sure of what you were trying to say, but if it's what I think it is, I'm hoping. I'm terrible!!! I'm just silly, that's all......

Do you really want a picture of me? Haven't they discovered another means of curing the hiccups in Germany? I'm afraid to send you one for fear that you may be so overcome by my beauty-fell face that you may go in a trance that will allow you only to gaze upon it and do no more --- like no more letters.

I'm not going to say that I must hurry off now, because actually I have about an hour to get ready to go shopping and that's plenty of time. I mean, what can a girl do in one hour that could improve something that has been deformed for almost 19 years. I must go now though, as I have a wash to hang and with my coordination, it may never get done. I mean hung.

"And although I much prefer writing to you, I must meet my commitments, mustn't I?"

Yes and no........

Love,
As Sometimes,
Always,
Maggathie

May 4, 1967

Dear Dennis,

Now it's my turn to apologize for the delayed letter. I was in Arizona most of last week and you know how it is when one goes sightseeing. You'd think I'd pick a place with class?

First of all, I want to answer your questions as best I can. I've given them a lot of thought, but actually my convictions were not made recently as I always felt this way. (Well, at least since I learned about the subject.)

1. Love is the giving of oneself to another. In marriage love is usually manifested through sex as two people give to each other all that is theirs physically and become one.

2. I don't know what kind of part sex now plays in marriage, but I have an idea of what its importance should be. Sex should be the second most important factor in marriage. First should be the ability for two people to get along and/or understand each other mentally. I do feel that sex is the most beautiful part of marriage.

3. Wow!!! Would you believe that the relationship between a Platonic love and a sexual love should be 50/50??? Actually when two people love each other they can balance this out by themselves for their own personal happiness. I would want to share in all of my husband's hopes, problems, and happiness as I would also want to satisfy him physically whenever he desired. I hope that his feelings will be mutual------

4. I don't think that you can really "know" a person until you've lived with them for some period of time. It is best that all differences be ironed out before children are involved, but I don't feel that holding off conception is the solution to instant happiness in marriage. I would not be unhappy if a child was conceived early in my marriage, but I hope that I will have at least several months to devote myself to my husband completely.

By the way, what are your viewpoints on these questions????

About the comment that you are so eagerly awaiting. It so happens that I am at work right now and can't seem to remember clearly which poem you are referring to. You wouldn't want me to make up some nice little phrase and not really know what I'm talking about, would you? So, Den, the evaluation will have to be held off until my next letter.

Arizona was really a sight for me. It was the beginning of many firsts for me--- 1. the first time I ever flew, 2. the first time I ever traveled with just a girlfriend, 3. the first time I ever stayed at a Hotel 9 with room service even!!! 4. the first time I ever saw a mountain, let alone climb one and drive on one, 5. the first time I swam this season, 6. the first time I ever went to an Air Force Ball, 7. the first time I ever drove stick shift, 8. the first time I ever saw a missile site, 9. the first time I saw a desert and cactus and the whole bit, and 10. the first time I ever took a picture of a duck. Honest!!!

Well, Den, I must get to sleep this time. One must get some sleep, mustn't one?

THE FAMILIAR STRANGER............

After May 4, 1967

Dear Dennis,

I just received your letter today. Since I have the opportunity to answer it, I thought it best not to waste any time nor take any chances. Question – What would happen if I let three weeks go by before answering a letter??

I don't want to sound submissive, but I very much agree with your comments on Platonic love versus physical love. Had I given this question more thought, it would have been obvious to see how true your explanation was and I wouldn't have to say "I don't wish to sound submissive." In other words -- you're right.

I remember your poem about courtship as it is my favorite. On the other hand, I can't seem to locate the "poem without comment." I found the letter with the page missing, which means I have it somewhere among my memories. Now if I can only remember where my memories are!

I'm at work right now---

Now I must get some sleep etc.?? I can't imagine how that happened unless I finished the letter at home. I'm a messed up person.

You can't imagine what this flat looks like. I'm in the middle of spring house cleaning and let me tell you, organized I ain't.

I wish you were home. Do you look forward to coming back to the states? I imagine you're thankful to have this opportunity to see so much. In fact, I'm worried that you may even prefer European life to American.

TRAITOR!!!

Now I'm insulted -- to think that a bar-b-que could come between us (sob).

1. Question – did I send you a picture of me?

2. Question – may I have a picture of you?

Guess what! I have to wash clothes now, so I must go, mustn't I? So there!!!

Write Soon

Somewhat forgetful,
Maggathie

P.S. I shall continue my search for the "poem without comment" until every clue has been investigated.

May 11, 1967

My Dear Dennis,

I feel terrible. You'll never know how excited I actually was when I received the post cards that you sent. To think that you found time to share portions of your adventures with me and I forget to thank you! Please believe that I am thankful.

It's a good thing that Europe is not where your heart is. I don't think I could stand the pain of knowing that you could never be happy in the U.S. again.

Answers to questions relating to sex and the marital state:

1) Personally, I feel that most men don't expect their future wife to be a virgin, especially if both are well into their twenties. I would imagine that men prefer marrying a virgin, but would say a man is unjust if he were to condemn a girl for something done in a weak moment of her past.

2) When I walk up to that altar dressed in white, I want to be a virgin. I can see that when two people really love each other it can become difficult to control passion especially if they see each other very much. I would not say it is wrong if it was a case of two people in love losing control. I do not like this business of "I have to see if we're compatible" nor think it's okay to use the body as a plaything for one's self-satisfaction - in other words, becoming a tramp because it feels good. You know, making sex dirty.

3) I feel that the Church should allow divorced people to remarry. Isn't it silly to think that a single or widowed person falls in love with a divorced person but is forbidden to marry that person?

4) I want to know as much of my husband's past as he feels free to tell me. Surely, I would not hold his past against him as I'm not marrying the man he was in the past, but the man that he is now.

5) If I were married and I had discovered that my husband had been unfaithful, I would find out as quickly as possible what was wrong with me that he had to turn to another woman. If it were a case of just a one night affair, perhaps he had been drinking, you know, well I'd be hurt and probably would overlook it. Do you understand that? (Let me tell you, I'd be jealous)

Well, Den, now it's my turn to hear your answers to these questions.

That's all – it's getting late and I haven't set my hair yet. You wouldn't expect me to show up at work tomorrow without a styled ~~couffuie~~ (oops) hair-do – would you?

Love,
Maggathie

P.S. Please write soon.

May 22, 1967

Dear Dennis,

Alright, Dennis, I'll confess. When I stated that I couldn't stand the pain of knowing that you could never be happy in the U.S. again, I simply meant that I can't wait until you come home and also hope that you plan to stay around awhile once you are home. See what happens when I try to be poetic? Let's face it, I ain't got no couth.

There's your picture -- I mean, my picture. I told you I'd send it, didn't I? Now, aren't you sorry you made such a fuss over that? By the way, it was my sister's picture. I hope you don't mind. I can't find the hundreds that I had made. (Patsy colored it).

I was happy to hear your echo. I get very frustrated when people get frustrated with me and my thinking. I don't mind differences in opinions, but when people try to make me see things their way when I'm quite satisfied with the way I see them -- they get me! I'm not saying I can't change my beliefs, but it bothers me when they have no respect for my ideas. In other words, I'm glad we think alike. You're one of the few who I can see eye to eye with.

Ask you questions? My goodness we've covered so much on sex and the like, I guess I'll have to switch to "married life and the battles of the intellects."

1) *How much time do you feel a husband should have to "go with the boys"?*
2) *Do you want your wife to work?*
3) *Who should handle the money?*
4) *Is man really the supreme being?*
5) *Do you believe in that saying "a good woman makes a good man"?*
6) *When children are involved -- who should come first, your wife or the children: or your*

husband or the children (if you were the wife) Confused?

Yes, I think I'd be happy to know that you spent at least one entire evening answering one of my letters.

Boy, do you know, you signed off with – "Strong Liking, Dennis."?

I was almost on cloud nine until I realized you were referring to your strong liking for the movie "Alfie" !!

Well, I guess I better go now. You wouldn't want me to give the impression that I have nothing else to do but answer your letters—would you! Yeah – I gotta count the cars that go by on the Stevenson expressway.

Love,
Maggathie

June 3, 1967

Dear Dennis,

I have been in bed with tonsillitis for the past 4 days. Now that I can get up (for a few hours anyway), I have no desire to smoke, or eat, and even my piano can burn at this moment, but I must write to you.

How can you be fond of a familiar stranger? Do you feel now that you know me better? – or at least enough to care? I'm not trying to make you commit yourself. I'm just curious.

Answer---

Fondness does not actually grow up -- but matures into love.

Echo time,

1. I agree
2. "
3. "
4. "
5. "
6. "

I can't help it, Dennis, but why waste paper saying the same as you only in different words. Let's face it - they were meatless questions. I guess we just about expired all the controversial ones.

I'm happy you liked my picture. My sister really painted that one up! By the way, it's your picture. Just don't go filing it away with the last one that I sent to you.

Did I tell you I'm taking Italian lessons? I doubt if anyone in my family will understand me as the dialects vary from village to village, but at least I'm taking a language that may mean something to me.

Well, Den, I think I'll get back to bed as I'm feeling a little quizzy (?). You wouldn't want me to have a relapse, would you?

Reread my letters? Why? Tell me -- what could one possibly gain by rereading my letters (or was it just a good excuse to end a letter?) (only kidding)

Lovingly
Maggathie

P.S. This letter really is an unforgivable mess, but remember not to judge a book by its author.
No! Don't judge an author by her writing? Forget it.

Yes, I do feel I know Maggie "*...better? – or at least enough to care?*" I know I do, but I'm not exactly sure how I really feel—at least not enough to admit it to her or maybe even to myself. There's something about Maggie that makes her different than any girl I've known and I want to tell her, but I have to be cautious. I don't have time to get into this today. I have a courier trip tomorrow and I have to pack. I'll just send a short letter telling her how she's someone very special to me and that I'll be gone for a few days to Athens, Greece.

As we begin our descent into Athens, the hydraulic lift for the front wheel of the transport plane on which I'm a passenger springs a leak, requiring the copilot to hand crank the wheel into place. This necessitates a layover while we await the essential parts to fix the problem.

The weather in Athens is "postcard perfect," sunny and 75 degrees, and is forecasted to remain so for the next week. The pilot and copilot aren't in any hurry to leave and decide the plane can't be repaired for several days. That's fine with me. I'll have several days in sunny Athens—several days to walk the streets of Plato and Aristotle, visit the Acropolis, stand on the ruins of the Parthenon, watch the changing of the guard at the Parliament building, and just soak up the history of Greece.

Four days later we are in flight on our return to Frankfort, Germany.

After returning to the Heidelberg courier station, I go to my in-box to gather my mail. I never get a lot of mail—usually a letter from my mother, an occasional advertisement, sometimes a donation request from Loyola University and, of course, a letter from Maggie. Waiting for me are several advertisements, a magazine, a couple bills, and a letter from my mother. Where's the letter from Maggie?

It's nearing two weeks since I've returned and I've heard nothing from Maggie. Every time Cpl. Russell distributes the station mail, there's nothing from her. This is unusual. She's been writing regularly and I just sent her a letter about my growing affection. I certainly didn't shout it out, but surely she can read between the lines and see I'm becoming fonder of her. This doesn't make any sense.

For the next few days, when he returns from the post office without a letter from Maggie, I ask Cpl. Russell if he's picked up *all* the mail. After a third day of this, there's a slight edge to his voice when he answers, "Yes sir, Lieutenant. I have, sir. Is there something you're expecting, *sir*?

Knowing my daily inquisition is getting on his nerves, I reply, "No, not really, nothing important. That's okay. Look, don't pick up my mail anymore. I'll stop by the post office when I go for my morning jog."

"Fine with me, *sir*."

I begin making almost daily trips to the base post office while two weeks slowly becomes three. Whenever I return from another courier trip and sort through my mail, I ask the mail clerk to please check again: "Are you sure you didn't misfile a letter somewhere? Could you look behind the mail bin to be sure nothing fell there?" He assures me he has done so today as he has at previous requests of mine—still no letter.

My mind is racing. Should I write another letter to Maggie? Maybe something's wrong. Can she still be sick from the tonsillitis? Maybe she objected to something I said in my last letter. Maybe she's losing interest in me. Maybe I was wrong about her. No, maybe she's just been too busy to write. That never stopped her before. How can she be so busy she can't send a short letter or a card? Maybe I should send a short letter or card to her, something simple like "Hope everything's okay," to see if she responds. But I don't. My pride tells me, *You sent the last letter*.

The fourth week passes and still no letter. The clerk at the post office is getting tired of my questions. I think he's beginning to feel sorry for me. Now, whenever I come in and before I can ask, he hunches his shoulders, cocks his head to the right, and spreads his arms out to his sides, palms up. However, I can't help but think he's getting some pleasure out of this. I stopped challenging him, but sometimes there's a silly smirk on his face. Certainly he wouldn't be playing a prank on me?

The guys at the courier station know what's going on and are getting a little annoyed with me. They seem divided into two camps: *Why don't you send her another letter if you're so upset about not hearing from her?* and *She's playing you for a sucker. If she doesn't want to write, the hell with her!* I let my pride win again and decide to wait for Maggie to write.

The fifth week passes. I keep thinking, *How can this be happening?* I certainly would have heard from someone if something was wrong with Maggie. Surely her sister would have mentioned something. I can't take this not knowing. I'm confused. I'm hurt. I'm angry.

I write a letter.

CHAPTER 7

ALMOST ENDED

Mid July 1967

My Dear Miss Maggathie:

To attempt to mask my displeasure at not receiving a letter from you would not only prove futile, but would be a comically foolish endeavor. I'm really quite perplexed concerning the possible cause of your sudden silence. Oh, I've fabricated numerous reasons. I told myself that perhaps you were still struggling with your tonsillitis, or maybe you were off on a vacation, or perhaps you sent a letter that I never received – and others, even weaker than these. But then the mind does something, rather strange and frightening. Perhaps weary of searching for new excuses, perhaps somewhat ashamed of supporting a host of anemic possibilities, it suddenly magnifies the one answer it has subconsciously been hiding – the now seemingly apparent reality that "perhaps she doesn't care enough to write."

I could have pretended I wasn't affected by the sudden cessation of your missives, but I decided to adopt the contrary:

I will tell you exactly how I felt. I once told you I was growing fonder of you with every letter I read. Perhaps this frightened you (if so, I think I can understand why), but, nonetheless, it was true. From about your third letter on, I must confess that I looked upon you as something more than my sister-in-law's kid sister. I was quite determined, however, not to hint at my recent discovery for fear that it might have been a spurious feeling. I attempted to feign indifference by hiding a growing affection behind a façade of witticisms.

But as time passed, I learned that the obvious craves to make itself known. This placed me in somewhat of a quandary – should I continue my role of cool detachment or should I trust the stability of my growing affection and express what I felt? I somewhat sheepishly chose the latter. Your reaction, a silence so ominous that it clearly indicated the death of an infant fondness.

I have reread several of your most recent letters and have reached a conclusion. I assume that you have stopped writing for one of two reasons: 1) You have become interested in some fellow and find little time to amuse yourself by writing to me, or 2) you have magnified some of my statements and frightened yourself into silence.

In answer to the latter, may I say that if this is the reason, it is one which, although understandable, is invalid. Perhaps you were afraid that I would like you more than you wished. If this is so, then I fear perhaps you suffer from the same malady with which I have been affected.

Perhaps you do have a poetic flare and placed on paper that which satiates your poetic mind, but does not necessarily reflect what you feel in your heart. I also have been guilty of this in the past, but too many sad experiences have prompted me to mollify what might appear to be a genuine feeling. I tend now to couch my feelings in less expressive terms.

Therefore, if you wish that I look upon you as my sister-in-law's kid sister, you need only say so. But, after rereading some of your statements, you really can't blame me for beginning to think otherwise.

The first reason – that perhaps you have become interested in some fellow and find little time to amuse yourself by writing to me – if true, can have little said about it.

The factor that gnaws at me the most is the uncertainty. I don't know exactly why you have stopped writing and until I am assured of the finality of not hearing from you again, I suppose I will walk from my mail box slightly disappointed every day.

I do want to thank you for one thing though: the experience of not hearing from a person you've looked upon as someone special. I've often dismissed girls with whom I have become bored in much the same manner. Just stop writing – the reason should be obvious. The sad reality is – it isn't. There's always that hope that maybe the next day---.

W. Somerset Maugham expresses it quite well when through the character of Phillip Carey he states:

"I should be miserable if I thought of her waiting and waiting. You don't know what it is to be sick for the postman's knock. I do, and I can't expose anyone else to that torture."

I ask only one favor from you now, Miss Maggathie, – that you simply tell me why you have stopped writing.

Dennis

It's been a week since I mailed my letter to Maggie. I know it's going to take a couple days for it to get to her and, if she answers right away, a couple more days for her letter to get to me. The earliest it could possibly come would be in five days, and if she can't write back immediately, maybe seven. I'm not going to go to the post office for awhile. Why go if there's no hope a letter from Maggie might be waiting? But what if she doesn't answer? I can't let myself think like this. Everything she's ever written tells me she has to answer this letter. But if she doesn't, what do I do then? No, it's not possible—she has to answer.

It's Saturday morning and the base post office is open from 9 a.m. to noon. It's 8:45 and I can't wait any longer. I'll take a leisurely walk to the post office to enjoy this sunny Saturday morning, but I soon find myself at a double-time pace. As I near the post office, I slow to a casual stride, afraid to find out what might not be there. What if there is no letter?

It's not quite 9 o'clock, but I gently push the entry door in case the postal clerk came a little early. It's open. I'm the first one here. The clerk is standing behind the counter with his back to me, sorting mail, and doesn't hear me approaching.

When I'm at the counter I utter a soft "Ahem" to get his attention.

As he turns his head and sees me, a small smile, or maybe a smirk, creases his face. "Lieutenant, where've you been? I haven't seen you in awhile."

Embarrassed to admit the reason I haven't been making my daily visits, I tell him, "I was on a couple courier trips and just got back last night."

He *is* smiling and it broadens as he says, "I think your letter's here, Lieutenant. I'll get your mail."

My pulse quickens at the possibility there may be a letter from Maggie. I want to believe him, but maybe he's wrong. He said he *thinks* it's here. How can he be certain? Maybe it's a letter from someone else. Every nerve in my body is burning as I wait for the clerk to return. *What's taking him so long? How much time does he need to go in the back, find my mail, and bring it here?*

After a couple minutes, the clerk returns to the counter with a stack of mail in his right hand. As he gives it to me, he's beaming. On top is a letter; in the upper left corner of the envelope—*Miss Maggathie Brown.*

I don't know what else is in the stack. I don't care. All I see is *Miss Maggathie Brown.*

The clerk continues to stare at me as if trying to gauge my reaction. I'm sure he's wondering if this is the long-awaited letter. I glance up from the stack, look at him and say, "Oh, good, she wrote." As if my feigned indifference is fooling him. He knows what this letter means to me and just keeps smiling.

I want to tear open the envelope and read it now, but I can't do it here.

I thank the clerk for getting my mail and turn to leave—to quickly go where I can be alone with Maggie's letter. As I reach the door, the clerk calls out, "Hey, Lieutenant!"

I snap my head around, "What!"

"I'm glad your letter finally came."

I sheepishly respond, "Yeah, thanks. I appreciate that," and bolt out the door.

Barely able to wait to get to the privacy of my apartment, I run the entire way back. Reaching my building, I burst through the entry door, bound up the stairs three at a time, rush down the long hall to my room, and fumble with my keys. My hands shake, but after a few clumsy attempts, I finally succeed in unlocking the door. Entering my apartment, I take Maggie's letter from the top of the stack, throw the remaining mail on my desk, and retreat to my lounge chair. After staring at the envelope a few more seconds to convince myself that this is indeed from Maggie, I slit it open.

I quickly scan Maggie's letter. My eyes race through each paragraph as I hurriedly move from page to page—anxious to hear why she hasn't written for so long and fearing she's going to tell me she's met someone else.

July 27, 1967

My Dear Dennis,

What could I possibly say to you to let you know how very sorry I am for not writing. All the reasons that you have imagined including – that perhaps I don't care enough to write – are far from the reality of it.

How could you possibly feel that your growing fonder of me could frighten me? Affection, concern, trust, fondness, love, or whatever are not meant to frighten – and surely, as I feel that I actually care for you, are welcomed when expressed by you. No, Dennis, I far from magnify your statements or frighten myself into silence.

How could you possibly like me more than I wished? Impossible!

Everything I write is sincere. If I ever really learned that you have doubted anything I've written, I'd be terribly hurt. Surely you must think "enough" of me to abolish the thought that I am a phony!

If your only concern is the uncertainty of it all, then I shall explain and hope to never hear from you again. If I'm really someone special, I hope that you will understand and forgive.

The reason is that I care for you too much, that I dismagnify your statements, that you don't trust me.

I have been writing to you for a long time – even before I last saw you. Time and again I've seen an absence of your letters only to learn that a Georgia Peach or college up in the up had taken all your spare time. Shocking to learn from a grapevine -- and very painful.

About a month ago, I waited three weeks for a letter only to be shut down with a "Hi, sister-in-law's kid sister" attitude. That's why I figured – what the hell. (Excuse me).

I'm not saying I want to possess you or have you writing to me every night, but it's no fun sitting in the corner waiting to be remembered.

There you have it--uncensored, perhaps uncouth, or quite foolish.

I'll close now. I hope you can take the time to think about all that I've said and perhaps understand.

As Always,
Maggathie
Your sister-in-law's sister

I read Maggie's letter a second, third, and fourth time, scrutinizing every sentence, every phrase, and every word. Two sentences glare at me until they burn on the back of my eyes and sear into my brain: *"How could you possibly like me more than I wished? Impossible!"*...*"The reason is that I care for you too much..."*

Every muscle in my body eases as I sink deep into the cushions of my chair when I realize Maggie hasn't met someone else and hasn't given up on me. As I sit at peace, a warmth races through my heart and covers my face with a smile. She "cares for me too much" Suddenly her weeks of silence don't matter anymore.

I have to answer her letter now. I can't tell her I love her yet; I don't want to build up any hopes I may not fulfill. But I can let her know she's far more than my sister-in-law's kid sister and she's the most important girl in my life now.

It's too late to go to the post office. I'll mail the letter first thing Monday morning.

I'm certain Maggie's going to answer the letter as soon as she receives it and I know I'll hear from her within five or six days.

Today is Saturday, the fifth day since I sent my letter. I go to the post office and find nothing from Maggie. On

Monday there is still no letter. Too embarrassed to go to the post office anymore, I tell Cpl. Russell that from now on I want him to pick up my mail whenever he picks up the mail for the courier station. Each day he returns with the station mail, I say nothing; I just look to see what he places on my desk. A couple times there are letters, but none from Maggie. The second week comes and goes with no letter. I'm not sure what's going on. Is she toying with me? I don't want to believe that. This is not who I thought she was.

I have to stop looking for Maggie's letter; I have to stop thinking about her. I volunteer for extra duty—additional courier trips and late night inventory—to keep my mind occupied. Yet, I keep hearing Maggie: *"...I care for you too much..."* A third week passes with no response. She told me she cared *"too much,"* then ignores my letter. I no longer know what to expect or what to hope for.

I only know that I've been such a fool.

Late August 1967

My Dear Miss Maggathie:

I sent you a letter several weeks ago, an honest attempt at explaining the confusion which surrounds my relationship with you, a sincere expression of my present feelings and future hopes. I expected some sort of response, at least acknowledgement of receipt. Nothing.

I am deeply disappointed in you, Miss Maggathie. You know, I told a concerned friend of mine about receiving your letter. He asked if you had explained why you stopped writing and when I offered your answer, he smiled. Just stood there with this silly smirk on his face as if to say, "Yeah, sure." I dismissed his reaction. Pushed it far into the corner of my mind with the accusation that he was merely a fool whose knowledge of a meaningful relationship was probably the sole product of cheap novels. I knew he looked upon it as a banal answer, but what did I care – how could he know if he didn't know you.

Yet, no answer to my last letter. I tried, Maggathie, to explain how I feel; to tell you what is in me without becoming too maudlin. I gave you the best, most complete answer I could. Yet, no answer. Courtesy, Miss Maggathie, courtesy alone should have prompted you to at least pen a short reply.

I'm a very proud person, Miss Maggathie, perhaps too proud, and I don't like to be made a fool of. "The reason is that I care for you too much..." I swallowed that, Miss Maggathie, swallowed deeply – swallowed because I wanted to believe it. I swallowed and answered as best I could, answered and received nothing in return. You won, Miss Maggathie, you've made a fool of me.

Dennis

It's late Friday night, the end of a long, hard week. Sgt. Upshaw and I are returning from a one-day round-trip to Munich to deliver a five-ton truck full of classified equipment. It's been a long, weary drive and seven hours on the Autobahn takes its toll. For the last hour I've been fighting to keep my eyes open. Luckily, Sgt. Upshaw is driving and he's been talking and singing since we left Munich. When we're within thirty miles of Heidelberg, I lose my battle with fatigue and doze off. I close my eyes for a couple minutes when I feel a gentle nudge on my left shoulder.

"Lieutenant, wake up," Sgt. Upshaw whispers. "We're at your place."

A little embarrassed and still groggy, I slowly shift my body upright as Sgt. Upshaw adds, "Look, just go, Lieutenant. It's been a long week for you. I'll take the truck to the motor pool and check it in."

Grateful, but too tired to do more than nod, I drag myself from the passenger seat, stagger through the entry door of my building, trip my way up the stairs, and stumble down the hall to my room. All I can think about is getting to bed. As I slowly enter my room, I step on a piece of mail that had been slid underneath my door, just one piece of mail—a letter from Maggie.

Suddenly, I'm wide awake.

September 5, 1967

Dear Dennis,

I am sorry that you think so lowly of me. I won't try to change your mind about me by defending myself.

No, Dennis, I haven't made a fool of you. I can't let you go on believing that and yet I don't have any real proof that I haven't, unless you believe in all that I have written to you.

I believe my last letter will be delayed although it is already in transit. It seems I put the wrong zip code on it (a terrible habit).

I must tell you that I am very depressed these days. My grandmother (more like my mother) is very sick and in the hospital. She will be operated on this Wednesday. I've just about broken every tie with my ex-fiancé, -- no regrets, but still painful to say the least. I really don't know what's wrong with me, Dennis. I really am frightened and so very lonely.

I'm sorry for pouring my troubles into your ear; I guess I just got carried away?

I'm flying to New York on October 7th (just for a weekend). I'm going to a convention that has something to do with my job (Quality Control). I haven't been filled in on all the details though.

There isn't much more I can say to you, but I just figured courtesy had the best of me and I must answer your ***last*** *letter. (Is that to be taken literally?)*

If I never hear from you again, I won't be shocked. I guess I really can't blame you for feeling the way you do, however wrong you are.

Please take care and stay happy always.

Maggathie

I sit rigid at my desk as I reread Maggie's letter several times. How do I respond to this? Every instinct tells me to slow down. The last time I hurried off an answer, she shut me out. I'm not going to be made a fool of again. I have too much pride and I'm not going to play the waiting game—not anymore. No, I'm going to take my time answering this letter. Let her see how it feels to pour your heart out and then hear nothing.

CHAPTER 8

ON THE MEND

Monday afternoon, just before lunch, Cpl. Russell returns from the post office with the station mail. I'm immersed in developing the courier trip schedule for the coming week and pay little attention to the items he places on the right-hand corner of my desk. After finalizing the assignments for the upcoming trips and making a couple phone calls, I reach for the mail. Rubber-banded inside a folded copy of my *Newsweek* magazine are several envelopes: my monthly car payment, a letter from my mother and—a letter from Maggie.

Wait a minute. I just got a letter from Maggie on Friday. How could this be another letter from her? It's postmarked August 29th. I'm scheduled to go to lunch in ten minutes, but I tell Cpl. Russell that I'm cutting out a little early and I'll be back in forty-five minutes. I hurry with Maggie's letter to the base restaurant and grab a cup of coffee and a doughnut. I sit alone in one of the far corners of the room, tear open the envelope and begin reading.

August 28, 1967

Dear Dennis,

I have no legitimate excuse for not writing sooner, but I do have several things to tell you that may grant my pardon. First of all, I'm in night school three nights a week (Italian lessons), my grandmother was very sick and I was watching over her as much as possible, I've been working every Saturday since the beginning of August for the overtime, and then in my spare time I've been doing the grocery shopping, and the housework, and studying, and babysitting, and just plain RELAXING!!!! I don't blame you if you never write to me again, but I'm hoping that you'll be able to understand. I really attempted to write to you several times, but I prefer much more thought to my letters to you than something scribbled in haste.

You don't know how happy I am to know that I mean so much to you. I wish you could feel the thrill that I feel whenever I realize this. I (a nineteen-year-old nursing school dropout) a candidate for the possession of your heart!! I never dreamed that this could come true, although I always wished that it could.

I always said that I would come right out and tell you what was on my mind, so here I go again. If I should ever make you feel that I am pushing you into a commitment that you do not wish to make -- please give me a good swift kick. I know I'll never ask you for your love, because then it wouldn't be love at all if not given freely. As for my love----you already have it. I'm not saying that it comes with undying devotion, but it's a more simple kind of love---just because you're you.

My goodness, you'll be home in almost ten months. I hope you're still looking forward to your return because I certainly am. Please want to come home when your time is up. (I sound like you're in prison)

Well, Dennis, it's nearly time to leave this place (work), so I'll try to get this in an envelope so that I can mail it on the way home. Be careful as I am worried about you.

Love,
Maggathie

Oh my God! This is Maggie's response to my early August letter; the one I thought she never answered—the one she sent to the wrong zip code. I read the entire letter three times and two of the lines at least ten times: "*You don't know how happy I am to know that I mean so much to you. I wish you could feel the thrill that I feel whenever I realize this.*" The "thrill" she feels? I'm giddy and my heart is pounding.

For the next fifteen minutes I sit alone in the quiet of my corner reading and rereading Maggie's letter and basking in the warmth of her words, far more secure in the stability of our relationship, until I suddenly turn cold with a frightening realization: Maggie must have received my "you made a fool of me" letter a couple days after sending this one. She tells me how excited she is that I feel as I do about her and I slam her with my callous response. What a fool I truly am. I have to clear this up.

After 5 September 1967

My Dear Miss Maggathie:

Today I sit in sorrow. Sorrow not for what I said, but for how it made you feel. You have been hurt and I sit ashamed.

What I said in my last letter was said in sincerity, but perhaps not to the degree it implied. I did feel a fool, Miss Maggathie, a tremendous fool, but not such as I feel now.

You told me you cared for me too much and then went silent for a month. If this is the rate of correspondence to people you care for, then I have a great deal to learn. When I care for someone as much as you implied you cared for me, nothing – neither school, work, nor other – nothing, Miss Maggathie, could silence me for so long. You can't imagine how anxiously I awaited your reply to that letter in which I tried to explain what you meant to me. You won't know how my heart sank when the days passed into weeks and the weeks into a month and still no reply.

Why. I asked myself – and I reread your letter – "I care for you too much" – but, nothing. And the next day I reread it again – "I care for you too much" – and yet, nothing. So, a month passed – a very long month – and I no longer reread your letter. I became bitter, Miss Maggathie, bitter with the possibility that you didn't mean what you said. How else could you remain silent so long? I was hurt and I wanted to hurt back. Not merely to hurt, but to hurt with a reason, to hurt so you would speak – speak and tell me how you really felt.

And you spoke, Miss Maggathie – spoke before my letter reached you. Spoke and told me why you didn't speak sooner. Spoke and told me how you felt for me. And I was happy, happy because you answered – answered as I wished you would. HAPPY – but only for a short time. Happy until I realized that you are now sad. Now I am ashamed. Your long silence no longer seems so cruel. You are sad and I made you so and now that is all that matters.

I said what I said because I was sincere: I said it as I said it because I was angry. I still believe you were wrong in not writing sooner. To justify such a delay to a letter of the sort that I wrote would be extremely difficult. I thought you wrong then, and I think you wrong now. But to strike back as I did, to say what I didn't wholeheartedly believe because I knew how it would affect you, was a wrong far greater than yours. To speak as I did because I hoped it would make you sad, merely to prompt a reply, was the retaliation of a man dazed with emotional pain. I was hurt; struck blindly – and now I stand ashamed. Forgive me, Miss Maggathie, for making you sad.

Affectionately
Dennis

The day after sending the above letter, I respond to some of Maggie's statements in her August 28th letter.

Early September 1967

My Dear Miss Maggathie:

If ever I feel that you are pushing me into a commitment I do not wish to make, you will know it. I said in almost my first letter to you that I would be honest with you, honest even to the point of hurting you. I will not be led into a situation which I do not wish to be led into, nor will I allow myself to lead you into a situation which I know I cannot or will not comply with. If I ever become aware that your feelings for me are far greater than mine are or will be for you, I will tell you immediately.

"As for my love --- you already have it --- but it's a more simple kind of love of you --- just because you're you." I'm somewhat confused again, Miss Maggathie. I'm not quite sure what kind of love you're speaking of. How am I that you love me because I'm me?

Correction Time:

"My goodness, you'll be home in almost ten months."

My goodness, I'll be home in almost exactly seven months

Confession Time:

Right now, I'm eagerly looking forward to coming home.

Possible Prospect:

I may be home again this year for Christmas. Much depends on many unpredictable events, but my request is in and the right people are working for me.

I must go now, Miss Maggathie. It's been a long weekend and my shoes aren't even spit shined yet. You wouldn't want me to let those ROTC officers show me up in front of my men now, would you?

Affectionately,
Dennis

September 10, 1967

My Dear Dennis,

Raise thy head and arise from bended knee for now thou hast pleased me. In other words, stop feeling ashamed as I feel fortunate that you did not give up on me altogether. I now understand why you handled this situation as you did, and I now understand you a little more – amazing?

Dennis, I've always felt unworthiness on my part in regards to our relationship. You're not just any guy who is exciting, physically attractive, intelligent and fun to be with. You're something special and it will take more than just "any" girl who is exciting, physically attractive, intelligent etc. to make you happy.

I doubt if I am that someone special. I'm not fishing for compliments, nor am I degrading myself. Perhaps this is all for you to decide, but feeling the way I do will always affect us until (I should say if and when) I am convinced that I could be something special.

Your letters have proven to me that you love to be loved, that you need to be needed, you're proud of your pride, and want to be wanted. I love to be loved, yet I'm eager to love, I need to be needed and yearn to need someone in return, I'm proud of my pride, yet perhaps I'm still too humble, and I want to be wanted, but I also want someone.

Perhaps I'm rushing things, but I cannot picture myself with you. I may not be your sister-in-law's kid sister anymore, but I'm still me. I'm not sophisticated, nor am I one who knows the right thing to do at the right time, and I'm ever so changeable. I told you once before that I believed I had a split personality.

I'm unaware of the types of girls you've known, but I might feel better if I knew where they had disappointed you. I'm not saying I'd put on an act to please you, but I'd at least know just exactly where I stand.

You've only told me that you see qualities in me that you respect and admire. What qualities? I'm charming?

I realize that I've never really told you why you are something special – and in turn you've never told me the reasons for your admiration of me.

One of the greatest things I've realized about you that singles you out from everyone is that I can look up to you. Don't laugh! Even my father, who I love and respect, cannot be looked up to in my eyes. Another is your understanding of me as a person. You know how to handle me, what advice to give, and, although letters can be deceiving, I feel that you can see through them and, in turn, come to know me. I don't mean that my letters are deceiving, but people tend to think before writing and when you actually talk to them they can give an entirely different impression. Honestly, Dennis, all of my letters are sincere and per chance maybe revealing the "real" me.

Now, I've really confused you and myself! I guess it will be useless to try to figure me out until time answers some questions.

I must go now. It's lunch time (I've taken all morning to write this -- my boss is out of town). You wouldn't want me to go on without "food" for thought, would you? Oh brother!

Love,
Maggathie

P.S. Write soon

September 13, 1967

Dear Dennis,

Why should you be so confused by a simple fact such as that I love you just because you're you? Haven't you ever felt that way about someone you've admired or looked up to? You're exciting, intelligent, fun to be with, physically attractive and sincere. Perhaps I'm not sure of what kind of a love that is.

My goodness, you will be home in almost exactly seven months. I'm happy that you're eagerly looking forward to coming home --- and maybe even for Christmas. Hey, how would you like to come with me to see how the Christmas tree looks in the Civic Center Square now that Picasso will have a part in the Christmas array?

I'm glad that I can be sure that I won't ever have to find out from some other source, other than you, that your feelings have changed for me. I'm not exactly sure of what your feelings for me are right now, but if and/or when they do change, it's good to know that I'll be the first to know.

I'm finding it rather difficult to express myself in this letter! I'm not sure what the reason is, but perhaps it's that -- I don't really know what kind of a relationship I'm dealing with. I guess this is really one situation when only time knows the answer.

Looks like I'll have to go now. It's rather late into the evening and I still must visit my grandmother in the hospital and dig out an outfit for work tomorrow, make a lunch, set my hair, shower and listen for the weather report at 10:15 on CBS. You wouldn't want me to go out of the house tomorrow with straggly hair, half naked and starving in the middle of a thunderstorm, would you?

Love, Maggathie

While on a four-day leave in London, I buy a small gift for Maggie to let her know I'm thinking of her. I include this note with the gift.

Before 15 September 1967

My Dear Miss Maggathie:

A small gift from London. Nothing spectacular, nothing to run to show your friends. Just a little something to let you know I was thinking of you.

With Deep Affection
Dennis

September 15, 1967

Dear Dennis,

I couldn't wait to thank you for the calendar. I'm really crazy about it and I'm already planning a spot for it in my bedroom. This way, I can fall asleep counting the days until you come home. Maybe I should wait and let you tack it up! No, not if I'm hanging it in my bedroom. It's not you I don't trust -- it's me.

I can't make this very long as I'm going to Dreary Lane to see the play "Generation" with Bob Cummings. (My girlfriend is an usherette there.)

I'll probably be writing again soon and I don't want you to get sick of me!

I really am thankful and ever so happy that you remembered me in London. The note alone would have sent me into heaven just by the way you signed it. I hope you weren't exaggerating or trying to stamp out that "ashamed" feeling. I know you weren't -- I think...?

Love,
Maggathie

Before 19 September 1967

My Dear Miss Maggathie:

This is going to be a somewhat short letter for two reasons: I'm almost out of writing paper and it's getting rather late and I still must pack for a four day trip to Munich and Nuremberg.

I had hoped that the more often we wrote to each other, the less confused our relationship would become, but it seems as though the contrary is proving true. "Why should you be so confused by a simple fact that I love you just because you're you? Haven't you ever felt that way about someone you've admired or looked up to? Perhaps I'm not sure of what kind of love that is." There have been people that I've admired or looked up to, and I suppose I could say I loved some of them, but those people were usually teachers, parents, or brothers. If this holds true with you, then I must confess that I am definitely flattered, but not in the least satisfied. I don't ask you to attempt to diagram your love for me; I only ask if I can hope it is more than the type mentioned.

What a lovely idea. If I do come home for Christmas, I can think of nothing I would look forward to more than going with you to the Civic Center Square and looking at the Christmas tree. I mean that in all sincerity, Miss Maggathie. I can still vividly remember the few hours we spent together last Christmas. How you kept me waiting in the lobby of the orphanage; how you showed me through the various wards, waking up your favorite children; how you oohed and aahed at my slides and was disappointed at the absence of ducks. I enjoyed myself tremendously then, Miss Maggathie.

I have a confession to make. I came home last Christmas to see my family. I want to come home this Christmas to see you.

Affectionately,
Dennis

September 19, 1967

Dear Dennis,

I won't try to hide my reason for writing to you at this moment. I am lonely, and for the first time I'm learning about the kind of loneliness you feel even when people are near. Writing to you seems as though I'm not alone.

I hope you don't mind, Dennis. I don't mean to push myself on you, but seek only peace of mind for a little while.

I wish I knew what is troubling me. Surely I'm used to the idea of being alone. If it's male companionship I long for, why don't I have fun with the guys I date?

I'm so filled with anxiety. Your coming home for Christmas is a thought that I cannot put out of my mind and yet I know, or should say -- expect that you'll be disappointed in me. I hope not, Dennis, I really hope not.

My goodness, I'll have you dreading the thought of seeing me if I keep discouraging you like this! Anyway, you haven't even asked to see me during the holidays. Anyway, you don't even know if you're actually coming home at all for the holidays.

About discouraging you -- well -- actually I'm quite charming and have many qualities to be respected and admired. Please don't be discouraged.

It's so wonderful to write to you like this because I feel so close to you when doing so. Never stop writing unless you feel an actual contempt for me. Even if your feelings for me grow colder, I still would enjoy hearing from you. I'm surprised at how close I really feel to you right now. Most people couldn't make me feel this way if we held hands!

Please forgive me if I've caused you to worry in any way -- especially if you worry that I care for you far more than you could possibly care for me. I'm fully aware of how I can be hurt and yet I'm unafraid.

Love,
Maggathie

CHAPTER 9

LOVE, MONEY, AND HOME

Maggie sends a multi-folded letter in response to my statement in my previous letter, "I don't ask you to attempt to diagram your love for me..."

September 21, 1967

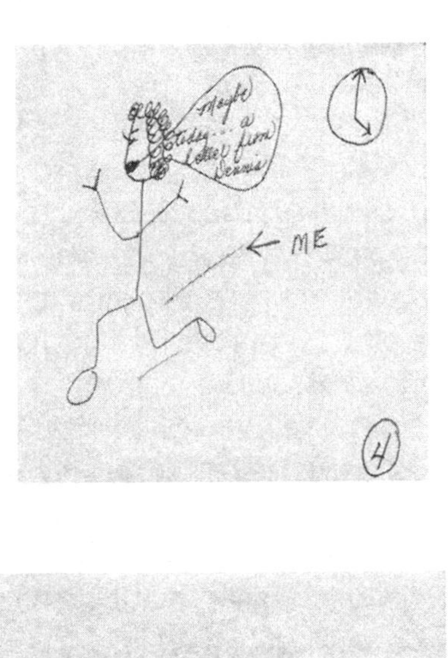
Maybe today... a letter from Dennis
ME
4

Maybe if I improve my grammar... I'll have a chance
with Dennis
ABC
AIN'T AIN'T A WORD !!
ME
YMCA
5

U
6

I LOVE YOU, DENNIS
7
THE END

Around 23 September 1967

My Dear Miss Maggathie:

Three letters in one week and each one more laudatory than the other. You once spoke of yourself as a candidate for my heart. After reading your last letters, I feel as though I'm a candidate for God. Flattered I was – more flattered I haven't been in many a year – but now I share your fear of disappointment. I will admit that I may be somewhat different from any fellow you've dated, but I find it impossible to associate myself with the me you spoke of in your letters.

In the course of attempting to build a case against yourself, you stated: "I'm not sophisticated, nor am I one who knows the right thing to do at the right time, and I'm ever so changeable." Are you implying that I am sophisticated, perfect and unchangeable? If so, oh, Miss Maggathie, are you going to be disappointed. I went out with a sophisticated girl once in my life – and I mean that literally – o n c e. I was never so bored in my life. Sophisticated girls don't like getting in snowball fights or skipping down State Street at night. What's a winter date without a snowball fight and a skip down a busy street?

About your implication that I might always do the right thing at the right time, remind me to tell you someday about the date I had when this girl and I waited in the wrong line for a cinema for which I had reserved seats – stood there for twenty minutes until I handed my tickets to the usher and he snickeringly told me that the show I wanted was next door. Or the time I took this girl to a restaurant at which I had reservations and ended up going to the wrong restaurant – and insisting that I had reservations until I discovered my error. How about the time I drank a toast over what I thought to be a fake candle. It wasn't. Rum and coke isn't as effective a face cleaner as soap and water.

So, you're ever changeable. Well, my dear Miss Maggathie, if you talked to your or my sister you might be mildly surprised to hear of my chameleon character. A person who is continuously in one mood makes me too self conscious. I begin to wonder if there is indeed something wrong with me.

Apparently, you're somewhat confused at my recent change of relationship toward you. It isn't really that difficult to understand. I never thought of you as anyone other than my sister-in-law's kid sister – your letters revealed qualities which prompted me to reconsider my concept of you. You are no longer funny little Maggie who I would occasionally run into when visiting my brother. You're not the high school kid whose crush I found flattering, but never considered beyond that. Since Christmas, you've become a woman to me.

I think I began to realize a change when I was home last Christmas. I never told you how much I enjoyed walking through the orphanage with you. I never confessed how I looked at you throughout the remainder of that night. I'm surprised you didn't catch me staring several times. Not a lustful stare – more of a confused wonderment. I felt my attitude toward you changing that night and I couldn't keep from staring. I never revealed how sorry I was when you decided it was time for you to go home. I really didn't want you to go. Let me finally confess that I was very tempted to kiss you. I believe I finally stuttered something about opening your door, then hastily retreated. Once again, reason ruled over emotion and I'm yet not certain if it should be considered a victory or a defeat.

Miss Maggathie, I'm not saying I love you – not yet. There's still too much to learn. Too much which can't be discovered in letters. Too much which can only be revealed in personal contact. Your letters have told me you're a woman, an intelligent, talented woman. A woman who knows what life is; a woman who knows what love is. I need to be loved, Miss Maggathie, a truth which perhaps could not be more obvious. But I have been loved, Miss Maggathie, by several girls – and that wasn't enough. What I need more, and what may not be so obvious, is to love. I need and want to love, Miss Maggathie. I want to give myself – my entire self – all my hopes, all my accomplishments – I want to give all that I am and all that I hope to be. I want to give love, Miss Maggathie, but the person to whom I give it must understand what love is. She must understand that it isn't only kissing and cuddling; it's sitting silent at opposite ends of the room, seemingly incognizant of each other, yet knowing that he is there, that she is there, and that love is the binding force which makes them one. She must realize that love need not merely be professed verbally and constantly demand the utterance of those three little words. She must be aware of the simpler, yet far more creditable means of communicating a love: a telephone call to say you'll be home late and not to worry; staying at home when the boys are playing poker because the wife isn't feeling too well; or bringing home the simplest of gifts on unexpected occasions to signify that you have been on his mind. She must know that true love is constant, that problems will most definitely occur, and that there may be times when it is difficult to believe that you are loved. She must be aware of these occasions, understand them for what they are (merely a passing phase) and react accordingly. The girl I give my love to, Miss Maggathie, must know these things, know them and appreciate them.

You stated that you would like to know where other girls have disappointed me and then commented that you would not put on an act to please me. Be what you are, Miss Maggathie, don't change for me. Hold onto that which is distinctly you.

Thank you, Miss Maggathie, for one of the greatest compliments you could have possibly given me: "I don't mean to push myself on you, but seek only peace of mind for a little while." To know that when you are troubled, you find peace of mind in conversing with me is a revelation which I treasure.

"Please forgive me if I've caused you to worry in any way..." Miss Maggathie, I'd never forgive you if when you were worried you didn't also cause me to worry. "I wish I knew what is troubling me. Surely I'm used to the idea of being alone." The longer I'm alone, the less bearable I find it. When I become accustomed to being alone, I had better begin making arrangements for medical treatments.

You weren't really looking for an answer to the question, "If it's male companionship I long for, why don't I have fun with the guys I date?" If so, then you haven't correlated it with an earlier statement you made, "...for the first time I'm learning about the kind of loneliness you feel even when people are near." It's not merely companionship you're seeking, Miss Maggathie, it's a meaningful relationship. Fortunately, they don't come with every knock at the door or evening on the town.

God – I talk too much. I'm afraid you're going to find that out when we finally get to see each other. You know something – I'm against television sets in the home. If there must be one, it will be for the wife's afternoon entertainment and special programs – otherwise off it stays. So much fun is lost with the tube on. None of my friends here have television sets and every time I go to see one of them, the evening is spent in relaxing conversation or simple games in which all participate.

You can't imagine how much I'm looking forward to spending an evening of conversation with you. Do you realize that we've hardly ever talked to each other – and never alone for more than twenty minutes.

At last you can rest your weary eyes. I'd probably go on for several more pages because I'm really enjoying myself, but Providence has taken pity on you – this is my last sheet of paper.

Thank you, Miss Maggathie, for a most enjoyable evening. The music was superb and the conversation delightful. I was wondering – well – I mean – you know – I mean – if you don't mind – well – I was kind of wondering if I could sort of – well, you know – stop by again sometime. I promise I won't talk so much.

Affectionately,
Dennis

September 27, 1967

My Dearest Dennis,

For the past week, the days have been sunny and yet, I was rather depressed and somewhat bewildered because I received no word from you. Today, it was cold and rainy, and all the way home from work I was glowing as if I could feel the warmth of your letter sitting there on my stairway. I just knew you'd come through for me! Thank you, Dennis. I've missed that love of cold, rainy days when the chill is succumbed by the presence of someone I care for. How much I missed depending on someone who I can trust. Only you could have made me feel this way today.

Dennis, how can I explain how happy your last letter has made me? Skipping downtown!! Dennis? You mean you aren't starched through and through? Wait a minute! Tell me you sing in the bathtub! Tell me that and I'll be forced to kiss you!!! How wrong I was about you.

No, Dennis, I can never put on an act for you. I can sing a little, and play the piano and organ, I can dance, but act? – Never, not even for you. I couldn't keep a straight face and besides that, I really wouldn't know which role to play with you. It is certain that when you talk with me for the first time, you'll be talking to me --- Mary Margaret Anne Brown the 1st.

I, a woman? I, a woman. Yes, I'm a woman, but I'm slightly unpolished and still rather weak at the knees. I'm glad that you're able to see that there's more to me than what I might show.

Yes, I remember that night that you walked me to my door. I remember that I felt that you wanted to kiss me, and I you. I remember the disappointed look on my face when you didn't and how my heart sank as you walked away. I remember how I longed to go to the airport and take that last long look at you. I'm so glad to learn that you felt "something" too that night.

I'm tired of hearing those three little words, Dennis. I'll admit that they are the greatest words to hear when they're said with all the feeling they imply, but how those words are toyed with to mean just about anything! I'm proud to tell you that I don't have dollar signs in my eyes. My favorite birthday present this past summer was a single, long stemmed rose given to me by our cafeteria maid at work. She is an immigrant from Poland, unable to speak English and making half of what I, a punk, do. She gave it to me with a smile and tears in her eyes. I love that woman more than anyone at that place. She's like my mother was.

Dennis, please don't think I'm acting when I tell you this --- I very seldom watch TV. I must confess that I'm fairly faithful to the 10 pm news and I will watch a motion picture on the late show if it's worthwhile. My favorite evening past times are (in order):

1. *playing the piano*
2. *reading a good book*
3. *having friends over*
4. *relaxing and listening to records*
5. *driving or walking just to see scenery*
6. *doing housework (if I'm in the right mood)*
7. *window shopping*
8. *writing (mood influences again)*
9. *sewing (I'm terrible at it)*
10. *going out on the town*

I could go on and on, but then that would really be too much! I guess my piano will always be my first love, but the other things can really shift around to go with my mood. It's hard explaining, but I think you'll understand.

Wouldn't it be great if things really worked out for us? Right now I'm filled with hope and anxiety, and yet both feet seem to be on the ground, and I'm willing to wait, and be ready for anything.

Oops – another confession. I like the cartoon shows on Saturday mornings. Sorry about that! I guess I'm all washed up!

I think I should end this now. I have to wash my hair before 9:00 pm (it won't dry by morning if I don't) and it's nearly that by now! Guess what? It's 9:45!

Write very soon and don't be afraid of talking too much. I'm not afraid of listening too much.

With Love,
Maggathie

Letter written on a note card.

Around 1 October 1967

My Dear Miss Maggathie:

Still no writing paper. When I go to the P.X., it's usually for something other than writing paper, so when I'm there, I invariably forget that which is most important. Perhaps if I tape an empty tablet to my forehead.

Tell you that I sing in the bathtub? My Dear Miss Maggathie, why do you think I bought a tape recorder - and a microphone with a capability of recording under the spray of a shower? Andy Williams has nothing on me. Why, with the shower running full blast, and the toilet flushing, I wouldn't consider myself too conceited to say that he and I sound somewhat similar.

"Starched through and through" Whatever possessed you to harbor a thought like that? It's rather difficult to skip down State Street when I'm starched stiff as a board. Of course, I must admit that some people have made a similar comment concerning my skipping. Then again, I never have contested being of professional status. Nonetheless, Miss Maggathie, I do demand an explanation. I have been affronted by your statement and demand full retribution in the form of an apology or a lengthy dissertation in defense of your maligned accusations – with the proper amount of footnotes and copious references.

I'm proud to tell you that I don't have dollar signs in my eyes." I was almost certain of this, Miss Maggathie, but it's somewhat comforting to be absolutely certain. It's important to have money, so it certainly isn't wrong to want it – but to crave it, that's something else. I want to make a decent living for my wife and my family. I want them to enjoy life and be comparatively comfortable. I want mostly to enjoy my wife and family and if the goal of a particular annual income will prohibit this, then I'd much rather alter my goal. I trust my wife and children will love me enough that they would rather have me home then be sitting alone in a $40,000 house surrounded by mundane pleasures while I'm out till unreasonable hours in quest of that insatiable goal. I want to give my love, my entire self, to my wife and family – not merely my paycheck. Oh, but here is where the woman plays such an important part. Here is one of the primary areas where the success or failure of my marriage will be determined. My wife <u>must</u> want <u>me</u> more than she wants that which I can provide. If I ever discover otherwise – no matter how late in marriage – from that point on our relationship will be irreparably marred. I don't ever want to see that time when my wife begins to badger me as to how much more my brother makes than me, or how much more I could be making doing something else. For years I've seen my mother peck away at my father. Peck and peck until I was certain that the only reason they remained married was because he worked days and she nights. I have discovered recently that the bond of marriage between them was too strong to be broken even by something as damaging as this, but I still contend that it has been seriously weakened.

All I meant to say in all this is that money is not my primary goal in life and I couldn't marry a woman who held contrary views.

Thank you, Miss Maggathie, for writing as often as you are.

Affectionately,
Dennis

October 8, 1967

Dear Dennis,

Enclosed please find one string to be tied around your index finger (right hand). This is to aid you to remember that stationary for you is vital to me.

Hey, Andy Baby, you can just call me Barbra.

Dennis, I'm sorry if I've offended you by thinking you were starched through and through. I know you're a fun-loving guy, but I've always felt that the side of your personality which dominates was an intellectual, book-worm type of thing. Dennis "the thinking man." Now I stand in astonishment. Now I stand at ease.

When I marry, home will be where my husband is. I'll give the humblest place a permanent look and be satisfied with anything that he can give me. I don't need sparkling diamonds, or a closet full of clothes marked "Marshall Field." I need someone to love. I need to be a wife and that's not possible when a husband works 16 hours a day. I want to grow <u>with</u> my husband and, in turn, we two <u>with</u> our children. A house is not necessarily a home. Two people bonded by marriage are not automatically "husband and wife." All the money in the world couldn't replace a man around to carry a heavy load of diapers down 3 flights of stairs. I could not tolerate my husband having every gift I bought him appraised or exchanged for a better buy. I'd hate eating every meal alone or the coldness of an empty bed at night. Nope, I don't care much for money. Happiness is living and loving without it.

Please don't forget to write soon. I hate to stop, but I really must.

You're welcome. Only you could stop me from writing to you now.

Affectionately,
With Love even,
Maggathie

CHAPTER 10

YOU HAVE MY LOVE, MAYBE

Early October 1967

My Dearest Dennis,

A terrible thought has occurred to me and I must explain something without waiting until I answer your next letter. I pray that you never feel that I have suddenly turned to you because of my broken engagement. How wrong your feelings would be.

I'll confess that when the ties between Bob and I were first broken, I panicked. I was washed up at 19!

About three weeks ago, I sat down and really looked life and all that it has to offer over, and realized that I had nothing to give to life in return. While doing this I also discovered that I have also so much to learn about love.

How foolish was I to consider marriage when I have so little to give to it. Not too long ago, love meant attention and security. Imagine that as a foundation for marriage!

So many doors have opened up for me now and my eyes are wide open. I know now what I must do.

Being born under the Cancer sign, I find it difficult to avoid being a home-body. The love and warmth that marriage can bring would be heaven to me, but I had completely forgotten about the person I'd be sharing this heaven with. Surely a man wants warmth and love, but now I know that it takes a little more than that to make a marriage work and more important to make a man happy.

You see, I know now that I'm in for a lot more giving than I expected. It's not that I mind, but -- well -- what do I have to give!!

To find the right man for me is going to be difficult and will take some time. So, please don't feel that I've zeroed-in on you as a new target for marriage.

Whew! I hope you can understand the point of this letter.

I feel that the only way to learn about love is to love. I have so much to learn, but then again, so much love to give and so much time to give it!

Perhaps this whole thought has never entered your mind, but if it has, or ever will, this letter will help to dissolve it.

My feelings of love for you have been for a long time. The one difference now is that they can "live" and perhaps grow.

Love,
Maggathie

Letter written on a note card.

Early October 1967

My Dear Miss Maggathie:

I would begin by saying that your prayers have been answered, but that would be incorrect. Better to say your prayers were unnecessary. I never once felt that you had suddenly turned to me because of your broken engagement. Reason: I was informed that you were the one who made the break and perhaps wrongfully assumed that that was what you desired.

I don't believe you: "Not too long ago, love meant attention and security." If this was all you felt when you thought of love, you certainly didn't mirror this in your letters. I don't doubt that when you thought of love you also thought of attention and security, but to believe that your entire definition was encompassed in these two words would be to deny the veracity of past correspondence. Of course attention and security must be showered upon someone who loves (attention in its many faceted ways) – how long could a flower last or how full could it blossom without the rain.

"...I know now that I'm in for a lot more giving than I expected. It's not that I mind, but what do I have to give!!!" It may sound somewhat corny, but you have yourself to give – and what more can a person give. If you give all that you are and are still not accepted, than you are giving yourself to the wrong person. So the only problem is not what do you have to give, but whether or not what you are giving is accepted. And you can tell, Miss Maggathie. Anybody who looks honestly at a relationship can see if their love is being accepted. But not only accepted – returned also. Again, as a flower needs rain to grow, so a love needs love. Even a slight drizzle, a hint of love, can keep a flower growing and a love alive until that time when it will be fully nourished.

"So please don't feel that I've zeroed-in on you as a new target for marriage." I have two answers to this statement – no, only one: If I felt this and objected, it would soon be made obvious to you.

"I have...so much love to give and so much time to give it." Does that indicate that you are trying to emphasize those last seven words? Answer me honestly, Miss Maggathie, is that for my benefit or yours? Does that mean that you have a great deal of love and much time to give it – to one person? Or, does that mean that you have a great deal of love and, being young, have a great deal of time to give it and, consequently, do not wish to bestow it on any one person yet?

I have a question for you, Miss Maggathie: what sort of state competition did you once win for playing the piano? I'm going around work telling everyone that you took first place in

State competition for concert pianist and I just want to be assured that I am not passing on erroneous information.

Another question: can you ice skate? If so, if and when I come home for Christmas, we'll have to go ice skating someplace. If not, well – I'm certain we can think of something else to do. That is – after we look at the Christmas tree in the Civic Center Square.

Affectionately,
Dennis

I wonder if Maggie will realize that my comment, "Even a slight drizzle…can keep a flower growing…" is my way of telling her I'm hoping her feelings for me continue to grow even with my modest admissions of an increasing fondness.

October 15, 1967

Dear Dennis,

I only have four pieces of writing paper left, so you may have to strain your eyes to read my fine writing, excuse all foo foo's and, pardon my frankness, and bear with me if I must stop suddenly in the middle of an intriguing topic.

Is it possible that you know me so well as to actually see my capacity to love? Sometimes I really believe that you understand me better than I. Of course I never believed that love was merely attention and security. The truth is I haven't been giving myself to the right person. I haven't met the guy who will accept me as I am. To my amazement I've also found what an important part trust has to do with love. No man has ever really put faith in me. When I speak of faith, I'm speaking of the fidelity type of faith. For some reason, I've been branded as a flirtatious butterfly and I'll never really know why. I don't gape at the guy in the next car when we all are waiting for a light to change. I don't return winks or rub somebody else's knee under a table. I don't have a list of the guys I've dated since 1961. I really don't understand why people might think I'm a spastic flirt! Putting two and two together, I've just discovered that once again the reason is that I've been giving myself to the wrong people! Thank you for telling me that. It's solved so many mysteries for me.

I have a great deal of love to give and so much time to give it. This means that one of these days I'll find someone who will accept my love and I, being young, have so much time to give it. As of now, you are the only one receiving my non-platonic love. I don't really know if you have fully accepted it. If in time you should refuse it completely, my love for you will probably turn platonic. I doubt if I could ever dislike you. If you should accept it, I'm positive that

I will always love you, that is, if I receive love in return.

I definitely am eager to give my love to one person. No one else will have it until you refuse it. This may all sound so ridiculous to you, but it is what I feel and consequently very sincere.

Answer time --

I was entered in piano competition for district members in 1963. (That means my competitors were citizens of a particular district of our State – I can't remember which district). Anyway, I was awarded the winner of that district. In 1964, I qualified for Illinois State Competition. This meant more pieces and more competition. I was awarded first place in this competition. In 1965, I entered State competition again and won again. My award was two full units of high school credits and a $1,000 scholarship at Mundelein College which I refused. In 1966, I gave up all contests and enjoyed my senior year. It all sounds terrific, but you must realize that the competition was limited to high school students. That's why I never really brag about it. I think it <u>stupid</u> to compete at the piano. My piano is my emotional outlet, not my medal winner or my means of earning a living. My piano is now my friend and only becomes an enemy when I must use it as a tool for success.

Do you see that number at the top of the page? And I have so much more to say! Rather than stop in the middle of an intriguing topic, I shall stop now and wait until I can find some writing paper. Besides I've got spaghetti boiling on the stove and my dad, home for Sunday dinner, is very hungry. Blood isn't really thicker than water.

Love,
Maggathie

P.S. Have I ever told you how very much you and your letters mean to me?

Around 11 October 1967

My Dear Miss Maggathie:

It is a somewhat lazy Sunday afternoon. The sun seems to be shining through what appears to be a completely overcast sky. I'm not doing much of anything today, simply sitting in my apartment recording some jazz albums. Had grandiose plans of spending the weekend in Luxemburg, but a little problem at work scuttled that scheme. Our inventory didn't balance Friday night which indicated that we may have lost a piece of classified material. A mild panic permeated the station. After two days of time consuming and tedious checking and rechecking, it was discovered that a clerical error was the cause of the mishap. A sigh of relief was exhaled by all, but I guess we had better brace ourselves for a lecture from the Major.

Went over Walt and Betty's house yesterday to play some Tripoley (Walt's a friend of mine from work and Betty, quite naturally, is his wife). I don't know if you have ever seen the game Tripoley, but if not, suffice it to say that it is a card game, which if played with pennies, is a most inexpensive way to spend an evening.

Miss Maggathie, do you ice skate? I can't recall whether or not you do. If so, and if we have time and if it's cold enough for there to be ice when and if I come home for Christmas – how would you like to go ice skating? God, with all those "ifs," I guess that was a somewhat loaded question. If just one "if" goes the wrong way, the whole question will have been senseless.

I'm very sorry, Miss Maggathie, there's so much more I wanted to say. It is now 11:45 P.M. and I haven't been able to write a word since 7:30. A half-drunk fellow officer stopped by my apartment and occupied my time till now. I care very little for this fellow and find it difficult to maintain a Christian attitude. But, I prevailed. I'll write again as soon as time allows.

Affectionately,
Dennis

October 11, 1967

Dear Dennis,

You don't have to apologize when time doesn't permit you to write all that you have to say. Although I prefer a lengthy letter, just seeing the words "My Dear Miss Maggathie" and "Affectionately, Dennis" is enough to fill me with contentment until your next letter.

I was relieved to find that the mystery of the missing classified material was solved. I would be left in shock if that episode had been the cause of a cancelled Christmas with you.

I'm very glad you came right out and asked me to go skating. I was beginning to wonder if your coming home to see me was limited to a "hello" and "good-bye" type of thing. For the time being, I'll forget about all the "ifs" if you will too.

I don't expect you to spend much time with me while you're home for Christmas. I realize that you're quite popular and you will have little time to do all that you wish to. I'm hoping that you will want to see me as often as possible. My plans for the holidays are limited to quiet evenings at home and old-gang parties -- engagements which can easily be broken at your request - engagements which I look forward to breaking at your request.

I must tell you about New York. I'll begin with my first experience at flying stand-by. My friends were scattered throughout the plane (I mean jet) and I landed in a window seat and right next to a scientist. He read such books as "the Chemical Analysis of a Candle" and "Einstein's Theory on something or other." He had a very quick tongue and I had so much trouble keeping up with him with only high school physics and chemistry to fall back on.

I fell in love with New York and was almost tempted to move up there in the Spring. Now that

I've thought it over, I'll first try it for one week to see if it is really all that I thought it was. I'm a silly person. I always dreamed of settling in some small community or even the country where it is quiet and clean and friendly. Now that I have no strings to hold me down, the brightness and brawn of New York has me in a spell of enchantment. Maybe it's simply a phase I'm going through.

The whole time I was there (3 nights and 2 days to be exact), I stayed at a friend of mine's house (is that good English?). I should say with his parents. It seems he was sent to Virginia at the last minute -- you know the Army. I really felt strange although I'm quite familiar with the family. Getting on to the point -- it is in the typical New York neighborhoods that you find what life there is all about. It's amazing to see how integrated even the suburbs are. No one really has a face in New York.

Flying home (stand-by) --- another window seat (luck) and the delightful company of a Hungarian immigrant. His philosophy was "grab and you shall receive." It was strange how out of the corner of my eye I watched him steal away with my helping of sugar, my salad dressing, my butter, and roll and my strawberry tart served with the United Airlines dinner. On the other hand, he was full of laughs and even sang a few old-country songs. I gave him a 59 cent box of meltaways to remember me by. He, in turn, handed me a silly looking red-stuffed dog with New York on the side of it printed in felt. I didn't want to accept it as it probably was for someone special, but he made quite a scene, so I did.

As always, it was good to be home, but I feel I must go back again as soon as I can, even if only for a day.

Well, I better get to work now. My father is home "visiting" and I must do his ironing before he ruins every shirt he has.

I'm awaiting the arrival of that "more to come" letter, but I won't hold you responsible if chances are that it may not come.

Until I hear from you or you hear from me again, please take care.

Love,
Maggathie

P.S. I don't mean that when I hear from you or when you hear from me you should stop taking care of yourself. What a goofy way to end a letter. I hope you understand that.

What does she mean, *"I fell in love with New York and was almost tempted to move up there in the Spring."*? What about our future? She once told me she couldn't wait until I came home; now she's thinking about moving to New York?

CHAPTER 11

NEW YORK, NEW YORK

Around 14 October 1967

My Dear Miss Maggathie:

I received a postcard from you which began, "I know this is nothing new to you, but at least you might share in my excitement." Suddenly I became a bit angry. You seem to be implying that because I have traveled to several countries in Europe, that I might look upon your trip as hardly an event of interest. My Dear Miss Maggathie I look upon anything you do with interest. If a trip to Joliet, Illinois was an event to which you looked forward, it would be an event of which I would be anxious to hear. Miss Maggathie, I don't ever want you to even imply that my past experiences might prompt me to look with disdain upon anything you do.

A few quotes from your last letter:

"I was beginning to wonder if your coming home to see me was limited to a 'hello' and 'good-bye' sort of thing."

"I don't expect you to spend much time with me while you're home."

"I'm hoping that you will want to see me as often as possible."

A quote from your letter of July 28:

"The reason is...I dismagnify your statements."

That, my dear Miss Maggathie, was perhaps the understatement of the year. Did I not say in one of my letters that I was coming home this Christmas to see you? Now perhaps I didn't say this exactly, but I meant specifically you. If it wasn't for my desire to see you, I wouldn't be coming home. This may sound almost cruel, but I have some very dear friends here with whom I would rather spend Christmas than with my family. I am coming home to see you and intend to be with you as often as courtesy to my family allows.

A Matter of Extreme Concern:

"I fell in love with New York and was almost tempted to move up there in the spring."

I'm glad you enjoyed your trip to New York. I have never been there, but I hope some day to visit it. I never had any real desire to see it until I gave several New York friends of mine a tour of Chicago: "It's nice - sort of a miniature New York." But there are so many other places I wish to see when back in the States.

It's getting late, Maggathie, and if I don't address this envelope tonight this letter might not be mailed until tomorrow evening. I'll write again as soon as I am able.

Very Affectionately,
Dennis

October 18, 1967

Dear Dennis,

I am very sad for I have made you angry with me. I honestly thought that you had already seen New York. I didn't mean to imply that you are a snob.

I turned that knife a little more because I doubted you. I really doubted myself too. I was worried that perhaps you would come home and be disappointed with me. My heart flipped when you said you were coming home to see me, but what if it became unbearable for you! That could happen you know. I honestly don't have any plans for the holidays, but I wanted you to be at ease to say "well, the guys in the gang are getting together and ..." It was wrong for me to doubt you, because I've not only lacked trust in you, I've hurt you.

Dennis, if you knew how I look forward to you being home, you'd have ignored those statements which have offended you. I dream and even worry about it all the time. My imagination is so very active that any slight or hurt will bother me more than it should. That's why I seem to be looking down about your homecoming. If I didn't and things didn't work out, the mental suffering of it all would be crushing.

About moving to New York ---- It all boils down to my need of security and something stable on which to build my hopes. If I knew that you did not want me to go, I would be foolish to even think about going. On the other hand, if I have no one to hold me here in Chicago, New York offers many new horizons.

Finally, Dennis, you have all the standards that I have ever hoped for in a man and letting you drift by or even to lose you as a friend would be a great loss. Whether you realize it or not, I need you Dennis and want you very much.

As of now, I've almost given you the impression that I am restless, changeable and even fickle, but actually when the right guy comes along, I'll be easy for him to keep. I will be careful in finding my love, but once I do, my affection will never fail.

As for my home life, it is growing worse. I always seem to be hurting those I love most. I sat in my hallway tonight and cried silently for almost an hour because I couldn't stand being in the house with my own father!

I'm afraid and lonely. I almost believe now that I do need psychiatric help. One minute I'm saying "Be strong, Mag, adjust, adjust, adjust." and the next I'm bursting into tears because if I don't, my nerves will break in two.

Please forgive me for hurting you. You must believe that I never meant to.

Love,
Maggathie

Is she asking me for a commitment? "*...something stable on which to build my hopes...*" "*... if I have no one to hold me here in Chicago, New York offers many new horizons.*" What "*new horizons*" is she talking about? Does she want me to ask her not to go to New York, to stay in Chicago and wait for me? I can't. I don't really know her yet. We've barely spent any time with each other; how can I possibly ask her to wait for me? No, I won't.

After 18 October 1967

My Dear Miss Maggathie:

Looks as though I may be spending a week in Italy next month. This fellow from work and I are planning to drive down there for seven or eight days. Hope to pass through Austria, then on to Rome and Florence. Other cities seen will depend on the number of days spent in the cities just mentioned.

Perhaps I was a bit too harsh in my last letter. I was somewhat offended by what your postcard implied, but I certainly didn't attain the degree of ire which you seem to think I had. I was angry, yes, but not seriously. Whatever anger existed was vented at the time the letters were written on the page. What I tried most to convey was not that I was disturbed at what you said, but that I was very much interested in all that you do. What I was angry at was not that you may have implied that I was a snob, but rather that you implied that I must not be interested in your every action.

Miss Maggathie, I'm afraid this is a terrible letter. It's past 11:30 and this is the first chance I've had to write all week. I'm rushing this and racking myself trying to think of something to say. But it isn't fair to you. I just can't throw anything down on paper when writing to you. I know this, but yet I must write something. I must let you know that I care for you and am thinking of you. Please try to understand that I can sometimes be so busy that I find it extremely difficult to write. This has been such a week. I hope to write to you again tomorrow – that is, if I don't have to work overtime again. I'm very much ashamed of this letter and the fact that I must quit without saying much of anything. I promise to write as soon as time allows.

Affectionately,
Dennis

Maggie sends a greeting card.

October 19, 1967

Dear Dennis,

Yes, I think of you constantly.

With Love
Maggathie

***

Maggie sends another greeting card.

Around October 20, 1967

Dear Dennis,

I'm out of writing paper so this card was the next best thing.

Really, I can't wait until you are home. I want to make you the center of my attention once you're here, although I may even seem like the clinging type of woman! I don't wish to make any demands on you, so if what I have just written appears as such, you aren't understanding what I have really said.

I have never met anyone who loves life as much as you do, nor have I ever met anyone who responds to my affection in the way that you do.

Love Again,
Maggathie

CHAPTER 12

FLIGHT FOR INDEPENDENCE

Around October 20, 1967

Dear Dennis,

Tonight I cannot sleep so I will "talk" to you in hopes that you are not sleepy. I don't have anything of great importance to say so I may just babble on and on! (By the way, I found this writing paper in my summer purse). Luck!!!

I must tell you that I am not only depressed, but very much in anger with myself. My father has come to live with me again and I'm not happy with this new situation. I'm not being bitter, nor am I still suffering from wounds he inflicted upon me when he left. I know exactly why I'm frowning about the whole affair, but everyone else seems to think that I'm a selfish, 19 year old punk who doesn't know what she wants. I first want to explain my feelings to you for obvious reasons --- 1) I trust you, 2) I feel that I can talk to you with a certain "closeness" and still you will remain objective, and 3) I know that any comment you may make will not only help me understand things a little better, but will probably be the best advice I will receive on this matter. My one desire is to refrain from boring you at any moment.

Nine months ago, my dad left this house to go on to a new future. It was then that I gave up the security of a textbook world and really started fighting for survival. Nine months ago, I began to grow up. With time, I finally rose to my feet. My bank account was growing (my, the almighty dollar!) -- no --- really ---. I began adding new pieces of furniture to my humble abode. I handled my bills (although a few were usually past due when finally paid). My time was my time. If I wanted to bang the piano, I'd bang the piano, or listen to Streisand, or paint my kitchen polka dots, or clean house at 11:00 pm.

Last week the roof fell in on me. His love didn't kick him out -- he merely has grown tired of his "restaurant life," so good old Mag saves the day for daddy! I love him, Den, I really do, but he's taken over completely! Not financially, mind you, but all of a sudden it's his house and I'm his daughter.

It all sounds as if I'm spewing venom with every word, but honestly I'm not. I just want my "own" little place.

Oh, I won't kick him out or hint my displeasure, but I have tried to talk things out with him and he, like all the others, makes a silly fairy tale or ridiculous joke about the whole thing. Believe me, I'm not laughing.

During the time I was really independent, I got myself into some pretty sticky situations. I didn't cry for help because I was always taught that once you've made your own bed, you must lie in it. Well, why doesn't that apply here!

I really pity my dad and perhaps that's why I can't really respect and never ever hurt him. Here is a man --- 55 years old. He retired collecting $165 a *month. $100 a month goes for debts which he built up helping Margo. Here is the man once too busy to come to his grandchild's birthday or communion day, or what have you, now looking for odd jobs and pining away in front of the tube. Here is a man who once – once? --- three times stabbed me in the back in the defense of hurting Margo, now depending on me (that 19 year old punk) for his food.*

I can't. I can't. I can't! I can't move away from this house and leave my grandmother all alone with strangers in the building! I can't tell Patsy that I don't wish to become involved with her problems. After all, she has no mother! I can't move out on my dad now, it would hurt him so.

Oh, Dennis, I know I sound like such a selfish person, but I just <u>can't</u> help sounding off this way.

You must be thinking I'd make a terrible wife.

Believe me, I realize that marriage is full of compromises and even that a wife must yield more often than the husband. This, I know I could accept. Marriage is one life being shared by two. What I'm waiting for is the day I can find that one to share that life with. As I am now, I'm like a puppet and everybody and his uncle has a string to pull.

I'm rather ashamed of this letter but I must mail it. I don't wish to hide anything from you.

I hope you can understand this and not think lowly of me. I will write again soon.

Love,
Maggathie

P.S. I feel better now.

Around 22 October 1967

My Dear Miss Maggathie:

Your father has returned and this has had an adverse effect upon you. The context of your letter indicates that you are "not happy with this new situation" for one primary reason: you have lost your independence and along with this your recognition as an adult.

It's a pity more people don't have an opportunity to be completely independent. There's so much to be learned in such a situation. It is only when you are completely independent that you are most yourself, and it is only when you are most yourself that you can hope to learn who you are. Some people claim that too much independence is dangerous. They contend that an individual who is on their own for a length of time soon concludes that they need no one else. After living alone for over a year, I hold the extreme opposite: it is only after living alone for a length of time that you truly realize how badly you do need someone – the right one.

Unless my experience at independence was totally different from most, I don't doubt that your first few months were, to say the least – extremely uncomfortable. The security of the nearness of people and of the proximity of their love was now gone. You were in a totally strange environment. Oh, the walls of your apartment were the same and Archer Ave. didn't disappear, but it wasn't the same apartment, it wasn't the same world. I hope I'm not sounding melodramatic, but when you are forced to live on your own, whether it be voluntary or not, you're forced to make "adjustments," make adjustments or forever flounder in memories. At first you feel sorry for yourself. You sit in an empty room and recall happy moments. You try desperately to maintain some sort of link with the existence that once was. You may even, as I did, when I first arrived here, magnify your affection for someone, someone who cares for you. You do it unconsciously. All you know is – here is someone who cares for me. And you need to be cared for; you need to be someone special; you need to be loved. So, you hang onto this, you hang on to the person who cares for you and you hang onto your memories – hang on because it's all you have. Then gradually, when month after long lonely month goes by, you begin to realize that memories are a poor substitute and that that growing affection is perhaps questionable. For the first time since you have been on your own, you no longer hang on to fading memories and spurious admissions of love. It is here the adjustment is made; it is here you finally become independent.

You have lost your independence and with that you have lost your recognition as an adult. This, I believe, hurts more than not being able to bang your piano, or listen to Streisand, or clean house at 11pm. Maggie, once again, is the sweet little kid who perhaps shouldn't have been left alone in the first place. Perhaps not, but the fact remains that you were, and you were left alone long enough to make the adjustment, long enough to become an adult. But parents find this very difficult to admit. You'll remain his child until you marry or until you reach the age at which he feels somewhat foolish to refer to you as such. Since you're still his child how can your apartment be anything else but his home.

Perhaps you realized before your father's return that he never looked upon you as anything but his little girl. The admission that "all others" make "a silly fairy tale or ridiculous joke out of the whole thing," indicates that you were aware that few individuals admitted that you had become an adult. But now the isolation of complete independence became a protection. Now the isolation was cherished because it was in this isolation that the truth was realized. You knew you were an adult and if you found yourself in a situation where those about you failed to realize this, you needed only to avoid such situations as often as courtesy allowed. You could return to your own apartment. You could limit the number of times you would subject yourself to such treatment. You could – that was until your father returned. And now "little Maggie" is "little Maggie" far more often than you care to tolerate.

So what do you do? Find yourself another apartment? You know your obligations; you know how far you can bend. You are going to have to live with your choice; only you can make it.

It's getting pretty late, Miss Maggathie, and I still have to prepare my uniform for work tomorrow. I hope what I've said has made at least some sense.

Very Affectionately,
Dennis

Maggie's Lock St. apartment. She lives on the second floor, up the wooden staircase on the right.

October 25, 1967

My Dear Dennis,

I want to write to you now, and at the same time, I hesitate. I'm afraid that you are still slightly angry with me as the letter I received from you today seemed as though you were so distant. It was not your choice of wording which caused me to feel this way, in fact, I guess it was like a sixth sense that detected this. Perhaps I'm still not myself.

I want you to know that I have my own apartment now, and although I'm still living on Archer, I'll be moving in about two weeks. I'm afraid it's still in the neighborhood, but far enough away to seek safe refuge. It's near 31st and Lock Street and I'm rather proud of it, although to some it may appear as a hole in the wall. It's really a lovely two flat with a front yard (complete with a statue of Our Lady). I live on the 2nd floor which consists of four rooms plus a bathroom (thank goodness) and a pantry. This is how it looks:

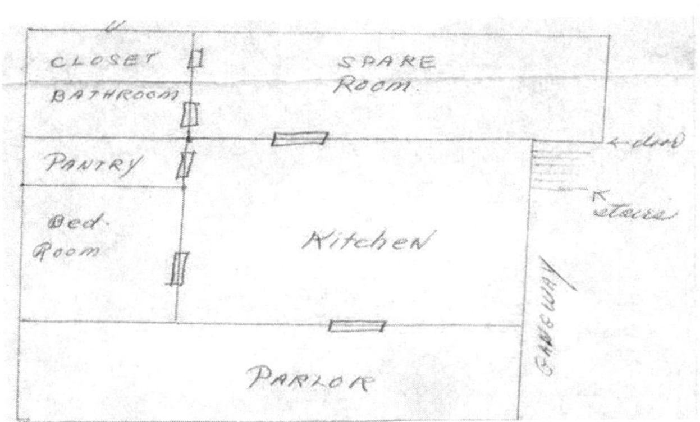

I drew that on a false scale, but at least you can see how it is situated. I'm having one heck of a time fixing the place up, but there's so much work to be done and money to be spent. I know it will all be worth it though.

My father and I had a good heart to heart talk and although the rest of "my family" thinks this whole thing is disgraceful, my dad understands -- and that's all that I'm really worried about.

I'm still holding you to the duty of hanging up the calendar that you sent me even if it must wait until March to be seen. You can rest at ease for I've decided that it will go better with my yellow kitchen rather than my pink bedroom.

How I wish you could be here to watch and perhaps help my apartment take shape. No one has seen it yet (with the exception of one close friend) and I plan on and have (so far) been doing the repair work, cleaning, decorating and furnishing of it all alone. Whether you're handy or not, only you would be worthy enough of sharing this excitement and happiness with me. Rereading that makes it sound as if I'm some conceited prima donna, but I think you'll understand what I mean.

Den, I must go now.

Love,
Maggathie

P.S. Please excuse this terrible handwriting.
P.S.S. I will let you know when to change my address

Love Again,
Maggathie

Wait! I must explain something. It may seem as if I asked you for advice and then went ahead and acted before hearing what you had to say, but actually I acted on two impulses. Anyway #1 was that I was almost certain of what your advice would be and #2 my breaking point came too soon.

Please don't feel that your last letter was worthless. Just knowing that you understand has set my heart at ease and it's such a wonderful feeling.

I don't wish to sound as if I <u>know</u> everything you're thinking, but I must admit that I feel that I know you well enough to know that you are very understanding. I confess that I had several doubts about what you might advise, but "something" told me that you would actually feel as I felt and act as I acted.

I tried to live with this new situation, Den. I really did. But it only took less than two weeks to really shatter my nerves.

I wish I knew if you're making sense out of all that I'm writing.

Something is bothering me. I've just reread your letter and I'm not sure if you are distant or not. This is about the fifth time I've read it and it seemed to have much more warmth than when I first read it. I still detect a "brotherly" attitude and it troubles me of all people—me who runs to Dennis for comfort every time I reach a crisis. I'm sorry, Dennis, that letter could not be more complete. I'm a silly girl.

Love Again & Again
Maggathie

Late October 1967

My Dear Miss Maggathie:

I have been in a rather terrible mood these past few days and I really have no idea why. It's been a very long time since I last felt this way. I thought I had gotten over my senseless moods, but obviously I haven't. Tonight, things are a bit better. In fact, a great deal better. Today I received a letter from you.

A quote from your last letter: "...the letter I received from you today seemed as though you were so distant...I guess it was like a sixth sense that detected this."

I say this without anger, but with sincerity: May I suggest you take your sixth sense in for a tune-up. Perhaps I shouldn't have said that. I'm so afraid you may take that the wrong way or perhaps think that I am angry with you. I'm merely saying that your sixth sense needs tuning up. I could not have possibly felt closer to you than I did when writing that letter. You must recall that you stated that you wanted my opinion because you believed I could be somewhat objective. Now, one can hardly be objective without perhaps creating a "brotherly" attitude. I tried to explain what I believed your problem was; I tried as best I could to be objective. I was sincere in all that I said and I said it with far more than a "brotherly" attitude. I am sincerely sorry if you interpreted it any other way.

I must be so careful with you. Everything I say seems to be given microscopic inspection – but I'm glad. If you didn't scrutinize every statement I make, it would indicate a degree of interest far below what I hope for. But you're not the only person who digs every meaning out of a sentence that might possibly be there. When I receive a letter from you, I try, if I am of strong will that morning, to postpone opening it until my work day is completed and I am in the solitude of my room. However, unless your letter arrives with the 4:00 pm mail, I seldom succeed in doing so. I read your letter at least twice upon opening it; two or three more times before retiring, and at least twice more before I plan a reply. Everything you say is analyzed and reanalyzed; every meaning that every statement could possibly have is considered against the entire context. And why? For what should be an obvious reason – because what you say means a great deal to me, and it means a great deal to me because <u>you</u> mean a great deal to me. I can't say I love you, because I'm not certain, and until I'm certain, I'll never say those words. Because until I <u>am</u> certain, that's all they would be – words. When I say "I love you," I don't want to speak with my lips. All I can say for now is that you mean far more to me than any other girl and that you play a major role in my future plans. I'm certain you would be dismayed if you discovered how much my friends know about you. Why, Henry and Cheryl have heard me speak of you so often that no sooner I receive a letter from you, they prompt me to tell them what you have to say. They are my very best friends and knowing how much you mean to me, they are naturally interested in our relationship

I want to say more about your last letter, but it's getting rather late again. I'll try to write again tomorrow if time permits. I've been kept so busy lately. I must go now.

Affectionately,
Dennis

P.S. "I'm still holding you to the duty of hanging up the calendar....even if it must wait until March..." Does this mean you're going to lock me out of your apartment at Christmas?

CHAPTER 13

"…I HAVE NEVER FELT THIS WAY…"

November 1, 1967

Dear Dennis,

It is sad that time did not allow you to shower me with attention in today's letter as you do in your past letters. Your letter is like manna from heaven to me.

Last night (Tues) I nearly starved for your affection, so I re-read every last one of your letters. It helped me a little, but the thought that your feelings may have cooled some by now kept haunting every word. Even as I read today's letter my heart sank because you signed off "Affectionately" instead of "Very Affectionately." Am I crazy…?

My apartment is taking shape slowly but surely. I was almost ready to give up, but knew that if I did, I'd regret it. It will be another two weeks at least before I move in. Now I'm really afraid of the step I'm taking. The place is still strange to me, but then I don't have my furniture in it yet. I'll miss the security of my building on Archer with its hallway and familiar neighbors. I'll miss meeting the same people at the bus stop every morning, and all the memories that linger on even though the appearance of this old place has changed since my dad moved in. My piano is not coming with me until the spring when I'll be able to afford professional movers!! (Need I say that I'll miss that?)

I must ease your mind and let you know that things are beginning to run smoothly again. Everyone has faced the fact that I am going, the apartment is taking shape, my grandmother is in the hospital under professional care, my sister has given up trying to run my affairs, my father has found a job that he enjoys, and I can start breathing freely again. I still have a rough road ahead, but with all of that off my mind, I should be able to keep myself on course.

I'm wondering if you've received Benjamen Leonardo yet. He's quite a character, really. You think he's bad, you better never see his mother Gazelda Louise. (If you haven't received Benjie yet, then disregard this until you do). That makes sense, doesn't it?

You know every bit of sense I have tells me that I am making a mistake by letting you know exactly how I feel about you. I suppose I'm supposed to keep you guessing or something like that, but somehow I can't do that to you. Do you realize that you're the first guy I've ever been completely honest with? It will be interesting to see how things work out. You do know how I feel about you, don't you? Need I explain?

Please be careful and please write very soon.

Love,
Maggathie

P.S. Dennis you're a dream.
(and don't come back with --- Maggathie you're a nightmare!)

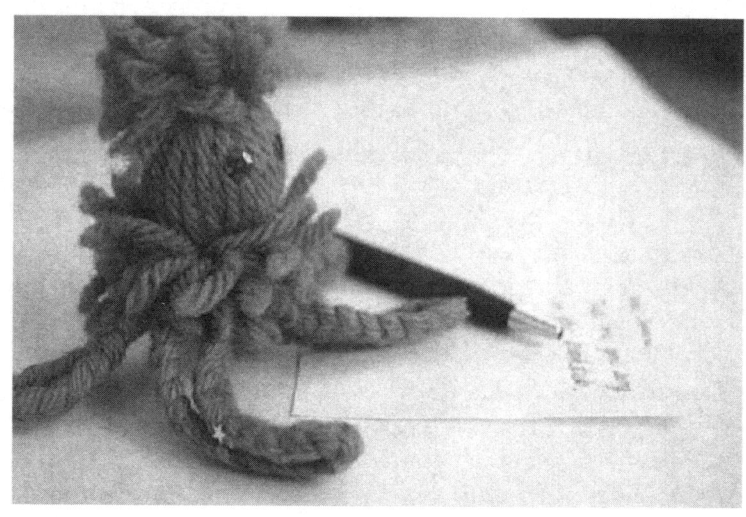

Benjamen Leonardo Auggy — the tiny blue octopus Maggie sends to me.

November 6, 1967

My Dearest Dennis,

Why do you feel that I may tire of waiting for your complete love? If I'm crazy enough to believe that there may be some chance for us, then I'm crazy enough to wait. It does seem odd that I may play a role in your future plans. It all sounds too fantastic to believe.

By the way, I have had my sixth sense tuned up and I've been advised to let it rest for awhile. I did feel that that one letter of yours was all but distant.

Yes, I do love you. It nearly knocked me off my feet hearing you say that I love you. I never thought you took my love very seriously. I've never loved like this before. My past romances started with a flashy courtship, soft music, moonlight kisses etc. You've given me none of these and yet, I feel that I love you. How? Why? Maybe that's part of growing up too.

Please don't think that I'm here tapping my foot nervously waiting for you to make a decisive move. Don't push yourself or question yourself so much that you don't know what you feel. I am here and I guess I always will be.

I always picture our first meeting at Christmas. There are two versions to this dream. In one we are on opposite sides of my sister's parlor. Nieces and relatives are opening packages and our eyes speak. That's it! Then in the other version, I'm sitting alone in my apartment perhaps reading, and suddenly a knock at my door. I walk casually to answer it and it's you – a strong embrace and then laughter. I'm a goof!!

I really must go now, but I vow to write more tonight. This is such a terrible letter, probably because I can't really concentrate between hellos from fellow employees.

Love,
Maggathie

November 6, 1967

My Dearest Dennis,

I vowed that I would write again tonight, but I don't wish to imply that I'm simply keeping a vow. I couldn't wait until my chores were finished and I could be close to you.

While working I thought of another thing we might do if and when you come home for Christmas. You must be my very first dinner guest -- Italian style. You'll be the first to taste my version of my mother's version of my grandmother's version of Italian spaghetti with meatballs.

How could I even think of locking you out of my apartment at Christmas? Did you suggest that because you found out you <u>*will*</u> *be home for Christmas?*

I was surprised to find that your friends know so well of me. My friends know of you, but I still can't really let them know how I feel about you. They've all watched me get hurt in my affairs with Bob and they're still too afraid for me yet. My best friend Cathy and probably my sister have guessed how I feel about you, but when I see that worried look in their eyes whenever I speak of you, I must run the show conveying a spirit of "don't worry, I'm not counting my chickens yet." I guess you're the only one who can accept my love for you right now.

This must all seem so awful to you and in a way it frightens me. Something keeps telling me I'm playing my cards all wrong, but then love isn't a card game. Yet, isn't it strange that I (the female) should be certain of her love and you (the opposite) so uncertain? Somehow I just can't picture things working out to a point of happily ever after. It just doesn't figure out right.

Let's see --- what do we have lined up for the "if" and "when" Christmas:

Ice skating--if possible
Civic Center--perhaps
Hanging my calendar--in the kitchen?
Spaghetti dinner--if you can survive
Snowball fight--not if I can help it. I'm going to get you by surprise and run like ----

I want so much to know that you'll truly be home for Christmas, but if not, I'll wait and wait for March to come around. I'll wait and wait and wait and I'll be the sincerest waiting girl you ever knew.

I must go now. I believe it is now Nov. 7th. Yes, I was right! Please write as soon as you can.

Loving you,
Maggathie

Speaking of the orphanage----?

I never did get you to see my very favorite baby. While packing I came across this picture and thought I'd send it. You may keep it if you like as I have others.

Love
Again,
Maggathie

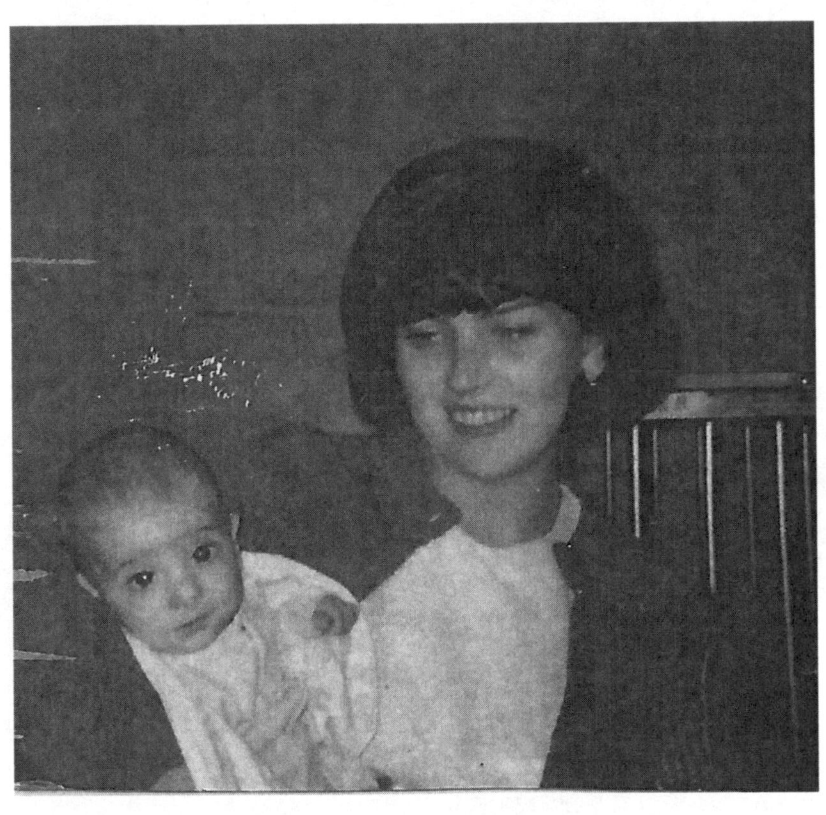

Maggie holding her favorite baby while working at St. Vincent's Orphanage.

Before 8 November 1967

My Dear Miss Maggathie:

Benjamin Leonardo Auggy? A blue octopus named Benjamin Leonardo Auggy? An octopus that is blue is difficult enough to swallow, but a blue octopus named Benjamin Leonardo Auggy is an impossibility. Why Benjamin Leonardo Auggy?

I believe I told you that I'm going to Italy November 11th. My plans are to go down via Switzerland, visit Pisa, Rome, Florence and Venice, and return by way of Austria, stopping perhaps for a day in Salzburg. I think I also told you that I was taking my car.

I hope I didn't make you sad with any of the letters I wrote last week. I wasn't exactly in the best of moods and I'm certain this was clearly reflected in my tone of writing. I'm sorry if I caused you any sadness or confusion. Perhaps I shouldn't write when I feel like that, and I considered not doing so, but I decided against it for one reason: I do get in those moods and I wanted you to know me as I am when I am in them.

It's rather certain that I will either be home for Christmas or shortly afterwards. Maggathie, I cannot begin to tell you how much I look forward to seeing you. I look forward to a walk in the frigid Chicago air to see the Christmas tree at the Civic Center and The Thing. I look forward to visiting your apartment and hanging up my calendar (I mean your calendar). But I look forward most to spending a quiet evening with you; a quiet evening of listening to you play your piano; a quiet evening of just sitting and talking. Christmas is only about six more weeks away. Six more weeks certainly doesn't sound like a long time, but when I think about it, it seems longer.

I have quite a bit to do yet tonight: shoes to shine, brass to polish etc, so I really can't spend much more time with you. I want to thank you though for making this another pleasant evening. You know something, Maggathie, I'm getting to like you more and more everyday. I'm beginning to feel somewhat guilty only signing my letters “Very Affectionately.” I speak of you very often and think of you far more.

I must go now.
More Than Very Affectionately
Dennis

P.S. Benjamin sends his best.

November 8, 1967

Hi, My Dennis,

I am very happy today and I feel as if I could explode with this happiness. Nothing is wrong for me – and why? --- your letter.

Benjie's name is Benjamen Leonardo Auggie because he looks like a Benjamen Leonardo Auggie, don't you think?

You never told me you had a car? Boy, oh boy, just when I'm really beginning to think that I know all about you -- you go and spring something like this on me! Well, I'm not going to tell you that I'm going to New York again on the 17th, so there! --- Well, I guess I better. Den, I'm going to New York on the 17th.

I hope you don't mind this snazzy paper, but my budget is at its breaking point so I have no other choice but to use it.

I am glad that you write to me when you get in one of your moods. Although I may have sounded disillusioned in my replies to these letters, now that I've realized why they may have confused me, I feel even closer to you than before. I want now to learn to recognize your moods, accept them (that's the easy part) and most of all to do all that I can to make you feel better even if that means just leaving you alone.

There are so many things I must tell you when you come. They wouldn't mean as much to you if I wrote these things. I hope you will be here for Christmas. I will feel very lost if you aren't, but perhaps just knowing that you will finally be home shortly will comfort that emptiness. Last Christmas was dreadful for me not only because Bob was away, but because I think I realized then that someone could have taken his place. This year I may feel lonely because you may not be here, but I doubt if anyone could take that feeling out of my heart unless it was you. If I were to tell you how very much you mean to me, you'd think I am crazy. In all honesty I have never felt this way about anyone before. I could list the things that make me feel this way, but I don't have enough pages of this notebook left. Even more, there is a special something about you that thrills me. A guy can be a wonderful guy, but it's that certain something that makes you fall in love with him.

Well, my Dennis, I suppose I may not be hearing from you while you're away, you may not even get this until you return! Whatever the case may be, I'll understand if I receive no word from you, but you must promise me a letter, a long beautiful letter, as soon as time permits you to write.

Love Always,
Maggathie

CHAPTER 14

APPROACHING STORM

November 14, 1967

My Dearest Dennis,

I must write to you tonight just knowing that I may not hear from you for awhile causes me to miss you so very much.

I am in my own little haven from reality tonight -- sleeping here for the first time. I am afraid that I am rather uneasy, but believe that I shall be able to relax with time. I can only fully appreciate my new home as only I know what it once looked like.

I'm afraid I'm still in that disturbing period of my life. I seem to be at bitter ends with everyone. I am a terrible person. I feel now as if the only way I can truly be happy is to be sheltered and protected and given my own way, petted and never opposed. I am overly touchy about my softness and seem unable to make a positive effort in any direction. To boot, I am overly anxious in regards to my future.

My sister has noticed how frequently you write. She keeps drilling it into my mind that you and I could never be. "Wait till he gets home, he'll be sorry." How can I win, Den? At first it seemed a joke, but now I'm not so sure.

I know what is wrong, but there is nothing I can do. Life would've been so uncomplicated if I had married as planned. I'd be safe and put out of everyone's worries! Life just isn't that way, is it? I could move to Hong Kong, but as long as I'm single, I'm still considered a scatter brain. Maturity comes with a marriage license? Poor little me; I haven't anyone to care for me. Poor baby.

I'm afraid this letter is awful and tends to ring with self-pity. I'm not aiming for pity, honestly. Let's just say I'm sounding off. Actually, at this moment I'm sitting back, waiting for "everyone's" next move, hoping I know how to cope with it -- not on the defensive -- just so "everyone" won't knock me down completely.

"Everyone" is right though. I do need someone to love and protect me as I am very insecure at this stage of my life. But where and when is the agony of it all. No -- who is the agony of it all?

I must go now before you call for men with a straight jacket. I'm not crazy, Dennis, just madly in love with you.

Maggathie

I send a postcard from Italy.

Around 14 November 1967

My Dear Miss Maggathie:

Bon Journo (or something like that). I'm presently in Florence (for two days) on my way to Pisa and Rome. The church you see in the background is the Cathedral of Santa Maria Del Fiore. My friend and I climbed to the top of the large dome – 400 steps

The fear I had of floods was fortunately unnecessary. There hasn't been a cloud in the sky since we arrived.

Florence itself isn't a very fascinating city, but the works of art here are more than compensating. Wish you were here to help me order a decent meal.

Very Affectionately
Dennis

19 November 1967

My Dear Miss Maggathie:

I have just returned from a long, tiring drive from Italy to the most heart warming “welcome home” gift I could have ever hoped to receive: four letters from you. I had expected one and hoped for two, but never four. Thank you for brightening what had become a very long, dreary day.

Let me tell you about a part of my trip to Italy. John and I started out Friday morning with the intent of driving through Switzerland and into Milan on our first day. By the beginning of the evening we had reached that point of the Swiss Alps where one has the choice of driving over the mountains or taking a train through them. A friend of mine who had recently returned from a similar trip had informed me of this juncture. He said the train trip lasted about twenty minutes, cost five dollars, and saved you perhaps two hours. He then added “If it's worth $2.50 an hour, I guess you should take it.” Well, John and I were working on a rather tight budget and decided that it would be interesting to drive over the Alps. About half way during our ascent, we ran into a rather thick fog. No problem though, we merely reduced our speed and hugged the white line in the center of the road. Then came the snow. Only a light film at first, but it later developed into about half an inch on the ground. No more white line. We now judged our direction by the mountain wall and the protective fence. Still, we continued onward. (One cannot easily extinguish the spirit of a Columbus once it has flamed so brightly.) Through the thick fog we now espied what appeared to be two parking lights. As we approached nearer we could see a car that was evidently in some sort of trouble. Being good Samaritans we naturally stopped to render assistance. It was an Italian fellow who could go no further because his car was sliding too much to make the climb. We attempted to offer what little assistance we could, but with his being unable to speak any English and we being unable to speak any Italian, we were finding communication a trifle difficult. After a short while, another Italian drove up. We decided to leave the two countrymen to themselves and proceeded on our journey. Proceeded, that was, for about two feet. Because we had completely stopped our car, we could no longer get enough traction to climb the hill. Still no problem, though. I had brought along tire chains for this express purpose. Since I had never looked at them before, and since John is a Florida boy who never even saw snow until he came to Europe, it took us an unusually long time to attach them to the tires. About a half hour later we were on our way again. That is, for about twenty yards. As we drove around a curve it appeared as though a snow plow had attempted to clear the road and quit at this point leaving about a five foot mound of snow blocking the entire road. About an hour later we were speeding under the mountain on the flat car of the train. Moral – some things are worth $2.50 an hour.

We drove through Milan and into Florence. As you probably already know, Florence is one of the cultural capitals of the world. We stayed two days and saw such prized art collections like Lorenzo Ghiberti's "Door of Paradise," Benvenuto Cellini's "Perseus and Medusa" and Giambologna's "Rape of the Sabine Women."

From Florence we drove to Pisa. We arrived late in the afternoon and only had a short time to observe the "Leaning Tower of Pisa." We stayed overnight and departed the next morning for Rome.

Rome was the first really large Italian city that I have driven in. May I be so bold as to make a few comments about your countrymen. If cars were built without horns, Italians wouldn't buy them. I don't believe an Italian can drive thirty yards without proclaiming his presence by a loud and prolonged "honk." Another thing, they have absolutely no concept of what the white lines on the street mean. One side of the road will be clearly divided into two lanes, but they insist on making three or four out of them. Oh, and don't assume that merely because a car is in the far left hand lane that he wouldn't think of turning right. He not only thinks about it, but blatantly does it. I honestly think they really believe that as soon as they turn their directional signal on, a steel barrier separates them from the rest of the traffic enabling them to cross unimpeded across three lanes of traffic. No sooner we found a hotel (an event which took an hour – how a major tourist attraction like Rome could successfully hide its hotels is a mystery I'll never understand) we parked the car and didn't move it again until we were prepared to depart.

THUS ENDETH MY ITALY TRIP

How stupid of me. Now that I look a little closer, especially at his eyes, I can fully understand why you could have named him nothing else but Benjamen Leonardo Auggie.

I'm very sorry that you were in the mood which your last letter indicated. I'm sorry, but I'm glad you didn't keep it to yourself. I only wish I was there to comfort you instead of making futile attempts via air mail. You can say just so much in a letter, but words, no matter how comforting, cannot replace a gentle hand on the cheek, a soft caress, and even a good cry on someone's shoulder. These moods will continue to come and while they do, all you can do is weather them as best you can. You'll continue to think such things as "Life would've been so uncomplicated if I had married as planned," but a sober analysis of the reasons which prompted your ultimate decision will reveal, in most cases, that you acted correctly.

"I feel now as if the only way I can truly be happy is to be sheltered and protected and given my own way, petted and never opposed." And by this, Miss Maggathie, you indicate that you are an average person. Who wouldn't want to be petted and never opposed? Who wouldn't, but who really expects it? Do you realize that the statement above contains one of the ideal characteristics of a perfect wife: "I feel now as if the only way I can truly be happy is to be sheltered and protected." EUREKA!!! What man doesn't want a woman who makes him feel that without him she is lost and helpless? Keep feeling this way, Maggathie, too many women today have lost this.

Very Affectionately,
Dennis

P.S. Perhaps you should begin cooking the spaghetti now. Upon my return from Italy, I was informed by one of my friends that the Major had my trip back home arranged. Now I'm not certain if it'll be for Christmas or shortly afterwards. I'll find out at work tomorrow.

Again, Very Affectionately + More
Dennis

November 22, 1967

My Dearest Dennis,

I was simply awed upon hearing of the experiences of misfortune you encountered while traveling. My hands fly up in exaltation at your courage to go onward. Surely you must have had much determination to put up with the wrath of the elements, let alone the wrath of my stupid "pisano" friends. I wish I would've been there, I'd let those Dago-Rootie-Kazooties in on a few things. Madone! I'm happy that all was worthwhile and ended well and what's a trip to Italy without a little confusion anyway?

I must say I'm a nervous wreck. I owe so much money that I think I sail for Canada in the morning. I guess I bit off more than I could chew. Actually, it isn't all that bad except that I'm broke and won't get paid until December 3rd and have just been greeted with a bill for a deposit from the electric company and dread to see what kind of a deposit I need for gas Friday. I get my stove and refrigerator (at least they're paid in full and make my household complete). So never fear, by the time you're home I'll be in the pink again and with my luck will develop some new problem to moan about.

Please don't think I'm hinting for money as I know I'll solve this somehow and it would only embarrass me if you did. Besides, you probably couldn't help if you wanted to. Now don't take that as an insult. I'm simply letting you know that I'm not really in trouble, but need at least one person to confide in. I believe you're the only one who really knows how weak I am. I can't imagine why I'm worried. I'm sure millions have my problem.

I received your postcard and was happy to know that you were thinking of me even in the midst of paradise. Ooops, I guess I'm exaggerating a little when I say paradise, but you can get the general idea of what I mean, can't you?

Do I seem flippy in this letter? I don't know if I'm hysterically happy because I've heard from you or just plain going out of my mind.

I really am happy at this moment: a warm, cozy apartment, a good cup of coffee, soft whispers of Barbra Streisand and a letter from you. What more could a girl ask for except that the "you" could be person spoken to instead of person written to.

I'm rather confused by your P.S. informing me that I should maybe start cooking the spaghetti, but I won't go into it. It'll probably be straightened out as soon as your next letter arrives. I believe it has to do with a mix up of words --- before and after. Forget it!

All I'm asking is that I see you. I don't care if it is just for one hour (yes I do), but I most definitely am anxious to see you whether it be before, after or good, old Christmas itself.

I must run now. I'm still not unpacked, tomorrow is Thanksgiving and I must marinate the Turkey (which is at my dad's house) and if I don't wash my hair, I'll be able to serve it as a substitute for string beans.

Loving You,
Maggathie

Around 21 November 1967

My Dear Miss Maggathie:

This is going to be a somewhat short, but very unpleasant letter. You had better put the spaghetti back in the box; I won't be home for Christmas – or for New Years. The attempt the Major made to arrange my trip back home proved futile. The circumstances are too complicated to explain so I will not even venture to try. Let it suffice to say that I will not be spending my holidays at home.

I can't begin to tell you what a disappointment this was to me. I had so looked forward to the several events we had planned. I was so certain that everything would work out alright that I had no intention of wrapping my Christmas gifts. I had intended to carry them home with me. But this isn't important. What bothers me most is that <u>we</u> will not spend Christmas together.

But all is not black. The Major is still attempting to arrange a trip home for me sometime in January. I hesitate to be overly optimistic again, but I feel very assured that his endeavors will this time prove successful. So, don't throw the spaghetti away – just sort of store it in the cabinet for awhile.

I want to write more, Miss Maggathie, but I am very pressed for time. I regret that I must be nothing but a bearer of sad tidings in this letter. As soon as the opportunity presents itself, I will write again.

Very Affectionately +,
Dennis

November 24, 1967

My Dearest Dennis,

If you knew how disappointed I am at this moment, you'd go AWOL. Just when I was beginning to think that things couldn't get worse -- Dennis can't get leave for Christmas! I feel hurt for your family alone, let alone worrying about the loneliness I'll feel during the holidays.

We do have a brighter side to look at. For one thing, we'll appreciate each other's company a little more. And there's a better chance for the ice-skating, and what the heck -- spaghetti's good any time of the year. Cheer up, Dennis, things really can't get worse. I told you that calendar could wait until March and I suppose I can too.

I won't be able to hide my feelings of sadness though. So very much depended on your homecoming that I find it very difficult forcing a smile.

I nearly had a heart attack before reading on after you stated that your letter would be unpleasant. I thought for a moment that you were going to tell me it was all over. I guess that bit of bad news will save itself for another month when I feel things couldn't get worse.

I honestly think sometimes that somebody's put the hex on me. Nothing is going my way at all. Next thing you'll know, I'll be in Manteno. Oh, I guess I should stop feeling sorry for myself. I know I'm lucky when I compare myself to some people. I vow not to make everyone's Christmas miserable by sulking. I'll feel the hurt, but won't show it. Now I'm making a real martyr out of myself. Forgive me please. I don't want to sound selfish, but at least you've got some idea of how I feel about you.

I have so many hopes about us. I feel that I shouldn't dream about what may never be, but it's my nature to daydream and be anxious about the future.

What really frightens me now is that I'll be a different person in your eyes when you see me than in my letters. It's one thing to have a guy interested in you and it's another to let him really get to know you. I'm almost certain that you'll be disappointed just as you were with the beauties I've watched you pass by.

I don't know why I'm so worried. Others have passed me by and I was rather glad of it, but you, you're something really special.

What respect could you possibly have for me? I write letters and all I do is feel sorry for myself, or degrade myself! You probably think I'm a real reject.

Good news! My stove and refrigerator have arrived. There's nothing to stop that dinner for two now. Now I have a real house. Just one more person - you -- could make it a home. Don't run, Dennis, I don't have wedding bells in my ears --- yet -- just the thought that with someone I really care for here, it could be a full-fledged "home." (Will you please calm down, I'm not pushing anything!)

I don't really feel like making Christmas plans, but I think I'll really go crazy if I sulked. I promised my girlfriend, Carole, we'd spend New Year's Eve together if you didn't come in. We'll probably join in on a party or hit the loop area. As for Christmas, I'll stick with the family (depression!). I was asked to fly to New York and spend Christmas there, but I don't really feel up to it and my family is more important on that holiday.

I pray that you'll be in during January, but March is close enough to dissolve any disappointment if you can't make it.

I feel that I should be ashamed for being disgusted with Uncle Sam. After all, we really owe it to him. I'm glad I was born a girl. All he can do is tax me!

Chin up, old boy, I'll do everything I can to make it Christmas when you finally do come in. I'll even, I'll even go caroling as long as there's snow on the ground. When you come home it will be Christmas -- for me anyway.

I haven't thought about presents yet (financially I'm embarrassed), but I'll do my best at giving you a present that money can't buy. The trouble is -- what! I'll think of something. I've got it -- and you're getting it. (Poor guy)

Well, I better get to my duties for this evening. Sears does a wonderful job of dirtying every floor, ashtray, wall etc. in the house when they deliver. I'm not complaining, I'm simply stating a fact.

Please pardon my disgust that I show in this letter. It's just that you're by far my biggest happiness and Christmas won't be gay without you.

Love,
Maggathie

One sentence makes me uneasy — *"I was asked to fly to New York and spend Christmas there..."* Who's asking Maggie to fly to New York for Christmas? How do I ask without sounding as if I'm suspicious? And still, I have no right to question her. I've made no commitments. She can do whatever she wants and go wherever she wants.

The continued conflict on the Island of Cyprus between Turkish and Greek Cypriots flares up again, significantly increasing tensions between Greece and Turkey. Diplomatic involvement of the United States and other allied countries escalates the flow of classified material.

Around 24 November 1967

My Dear Miss Maggathie:

Forgive me. Again I must write a short letter. I have received two letters from you in as many days and I do not have the time to properly answer one of them. The turmoil between Turkey and Greece has placed a burden upon our station which greatly limits my free time.

Tomorrow I must go to Munich on business. I'm afraid I won't be able to write to you until this week-end.

I want so badly to write. There are so many things I want to say to you. You have sounded so dejected in parts of your last two letters and time allows me to do nothing else but accept your moods and idly stand by. How utterly helpless I feel.

I don't feel very well tonight; my legs are weak and I seem to have a fever. Wouldn't you know it? Today I get the first flu shot I've had in three years and I'm probably catching the flu.

God – these last two letters I've written must really be cheering you up. I'm sorry, Miss Maggathie, honestly I am. I'll make it up to you this weekend.

Most Affectionately,
Dennis

P.S. You didn't tell me about your trip to New York. Please do.
P.P.S. Please don't stop dreaming or being anxious about the future
P.P.P.S. I'm sorry, Miss Maggathie, I must go.
P.P.P.P.S. Write soon. I need your letters.

November 27, 1967

My Dearest Dennis,

My grandmother is dead. Forgive me for writing this so bluntly, but I sat there and watched and lived through her "death rattle" and now she is dead.

I'm frightened and dazed, not so much because of death itself, but because I have lost her, the one who loved me most of all. I was her favorite, for me she would've died and I gave her -- nothing and now she is gone. Every creak in the woodwork, every chill in the air I feel causes me to be frightened and heightens a desire to run, but where?

And things couldn't have gotten any worse just two days ago! How I need you now! As much as I try not to force you into commitment, I sincerely need you now whether you would wish to help me or not. I believe you would. If you were here, I would feel at least half-human and half-myself. Would you? Could you? I am not worthy of you. I must stop this dreaming.

So much lies ahead. Arguments over "who" gets "what," "who" did this much and "who" did that much and already they (her children) have grabbed the unclaimed. I've been cast aside. I should say that I have seeped into the scenery. I am nothing. Why and how can they look at the "what do we get" side of it?

There's a will. My name is mentioned and yet I won't hear it. I can't. It won't be "real" to me.

Something not in the will—wedding rings -- promised to me so that together with my mother's would make one ring and with my rings -- one ring for my daughter, but someone has them. I know who it is, yet I am afraid to stake a claim. Do I dare think of a sentimental value? I'm just a granddaughter – yet, I was the favorite. I loved her, yes, and to me she will always be somewhat alive in my heart. I don't need rings, do I?

I'll always remember the stories she told me of life. Her own little parables that were funny in broken English and yet so face slapping full of truth.

No one will ever cook like she did. My spaghetti will never even come close to the banquet she made out of noodles and a little tomato paste. I haven't got the magic she had in her cooking.

That summer cottage in Lake Geneva can go to blazes. Without sunshine flowers all around, the smell of good warm homemade bread, and the chuckles of her and her "old-country" friends, it will be a countryside motel unlike the place I knew as a summer home.

I'm glad I am away from the building on Archer. Certainly it will go to the dogs. No one will make the hallway smell bleachy clean, and no one will be there to sew up a loose hem at a moment's notice, or give me a hard fight about how stiff my hair is.

At the very end my uncle gave a speech and mentioned that it was I, above all, even her own children, that she loved and worried about most. She told me that living or dead, she would take care of me.

Perhaps she will take care of me now. I hope so. I need to be taken care of by someone. I don't want to go on alone anymore. I am afraid and tired of fighting alone. I'm going to find someone to love me. I'll know it when it comes because when I look into a pair of eyes that are one with mine in love, I won't be able to see them because they'll almost be my eyes. I must leave you. No more dreams.

Maggathie

CHAPTER 15

WAKE-UP CALL

Maggie's grandmother is dead. She's lost another "mother" and I can do nothing. She's in such pain and here I sit, an ocean apart, unable to do anything but put some words on paper to try to comfort her.

Early December 1967

My Dear Miss Maggathie:

It is at times like this that one fully realizes how limited words can be. Any phrase I might use to attempt to express my condolences seems so banal – so empty. What am I to say?

In all honesty, I cannot feel what you feel. I have never experienced the loss of someone so dear to me. I can only hope to understand, and in my understanding, hope to share in your loss.

You have lost a second mother and, grief stricken, turn for a shoulder to lean on. And all I can offer is a few simple sentences; a frail attempt to salve your pain. One can't lean too heavily on a sheet of paper.

I feel so utterly useless. You are so sad and so desperately in need of someone and I can do nothing. I can only sit, an ocean apart, and attempt to convince you that you are not alone; that the void you feel is shared by someone who cares very much for you. I can only say that I want so badly to be by your side so that you may rest your head upon my shoulder and cry until the tears refuse to come; so that I may hold you near, hold you so near and so tight that you would gain a degree of comfort from knowing that there is someone upon whom you can depend. I can only say this and do no more. And because I can only say this, I feel as though I have failed you. The time has come when you need me most, need me, not simply words, and I can do nothing.

Dennis

I'm shaken to my core—not solely because Maggie's grandmother died; not only because of the grief Maggie is suffering; and not because I can't do much to comfort her. No, I'm shaken more by the way she ends her letter *"I'm going to find someone to love me… I must leave you. No more dreams."*

I'm afraid Maggie's given up on me. I know these past few weeks have been very difficult for her: living on her own, feeling frightened and lonely, her mounting bills, her sister telling her she has no chance with me and Maggie believing it, my guardedly expressing my feelings for her, my not coming home for Christmas, my sending two very short letters at a time she's feeling so low—and now her grandmother's death.

I can't let her give up on me.

(Two days later)
Early December 1967

My Dear Miss Maggathie:

I am terribly depressed. The last sentence of your most recent letter has greatly saddened me. Three little words and their implication has cast a dolorous shadow upon any future plans I may have envisioned. "No more dreams," and by this you imply that you have lost hope in me. "No more dreams" is to say "We don't stand a chance. I cannot continue for four months without being certain of how it will end. I will not wait."

What am I to do, Miss Maggathie? You have stated in previous letters that you do not wish to force me into a commitment, yet what am I to do when I'm faced with the possibility of losing you? What am I to do when the only girl who means anything to me says, "I must have an answer – now. I cannot wait." What am I to do when it is impossible to give this answer?

You don't know, Miss Maggathie, the almost psychotic fear I have of saying "I love you." The word "love" is so fraught with meaning, so fraught with responsibilities that I dare not utter it until I am certain. When I say "I love you," it won't simply imply that I find you physically and mentally attractive or that I place you above any other girl – it will mean far more than this. When I say "I love you," it will mean I want you for my wife; I want you to be the mother of my children; I want you to stand by my side as long as life permits. It will mean that you are the one who complements me, who makes me whole. When I say "I love you," it will mean that my life is yours. Everything I do, everything I hope to do, all my wildest dreams, all my fondest desires are for you. When I say "I love you," it will mean that there <u>is</u> no other and far more important, that there <u>will be</u> no other. This is why I must be certain. This is why I cannot speak; why I must couch my feelings in hidden phrases. Please try to understand, Miss Maggathie – you must.

"I must leave you. No more dreams." Every time I read that, Miss Maggathie, every time I grasp the full implications of those last three words, I feel a numbness which frightens me. I don't want you to stop dreaming, Miss Maggathie, for from your dreams arise my hopes.

"I'm almost certain that you'll be disappointed just as you were with the beauties I've watched you pass by." (Nov. 24)

Speaking of your sister – "She keeps drilling it into my mind that you and I could never be...At first it seemed a joke, but now I'm not so sure." (Nov 14)

"...but the thought that your feelings may have cooled some by now kept haunting every word. Even as I read today's letter, my heart sank because you signed off 'Affectionately' instead of 'Very Affectionately' Am I crazy?" (Nov 1) (Yes, Miss Maggathie, you are.)

"I thought ... you were going to tell me it was all over. I guess that bit of bad news will save itself for another month when I feel things couldn't get worse." (Nov 24)

"I am not worthy of you." (Nov 27)

Such comments have been far too common. At first I concluded that you were perhaps in such a mood which fosters such remarks, but the regularity of them has prompted me to think otherwise. If you honestly believe that we could never be one because I am too good for you, then you do us both a grave injustice. As flattered as I have been with your many compliments, Miss Maggathie, I am not the man you think I am. Why you have fallen so in love with me is something I cannot understand, and why you see me as you do is more than reason enough for me to accept the credibility of the adage "Love is blind." It is not you who should fear my disappointment, but rather I who should fear yours. And I do, Miss Maggathie, more than you can imagine. You have placed me upon a pedestal, a pedestal upon which I may find it impossible to maintain my balance. I'm frightened of such heights, Miss Maggathie, frightened of falling and shattering the image you have of me.

"I don't want to go on alone anymore. I am afraid and tired of fighting alone." I am saddened to think that you feel this way. If you feel that you have faced your problems by yourself; if you truly believe that you have stood with no one by your side, then I have suffered in vain. I have failed you again. You turned to me when you were troubled and I failed to convince you that I was concerned; that I was happy when you were happy, sad when you were sad; that what you felt, I felt – that you were not alone. If I have failed you in this, then I could not have failed you more seriously. If I have failed you in this, I do not deserve your love.

Maggathie, you signed your last letter simply "Maggathie." Promise me you'll never sign without "Love" again. Please.

Very Affectionately,
Dennis

December 4, 1967

My Dearest Dennis,

I had intended on forgetting about you. But just as the doubt of the future tells me to find someone else, so does my love for you tell me that I must wait until I am sure there is nothing to hope for. I know you've said many things to me which mean so very much. That you care for me far more than any other girl, that I may play a major role in your future plans, that your Christmas will be ruined mainly because <u>we</u> will not be spending it together... There is so much that I should be grateful for. So many things you've said and meant without even spending as much as one evening with me, and still I feel that I need more, much more than that.

It probably all comes down to all the problems I've had recently. I don't think I can take much more. With everything going badly and no one there who really cares, it all isn't easy to accept. I admit that my family and friends have cared and helped me in many ways, but I guess financial aid and good advice are still far less than what I'm searching for.

You've thrown me off by telling me not to stop being anxious about the future. Perhaps you didn't realize how much you're involved in that future. If you did realize I was referring to you, then for heaven's sake please don't build my hopes up only to send me crashing toward a heart break.

I can't help myself, Dennis. I am really in love with you. My romantic life is thrilling, flashy, and even warmed with true loves, but I can give nothing in return as you and only you have my all. I don't know what to do anymore.

It's not that you don't write often enough, and it's not that you're far away. My doubts are your doubts. What more can I say? I realize that I am or seem to be pushing you and how I despise myself for acting this way.

I have just reread all that I have written so far. It seems as if I've asked you to make a choice, but I'm not sure if that's what I want. Perhaps if you did make a choice, I'd lose you. I keep telling myself not to mail this letter. I know it's a terrible letter, but it's the way I feel, almost naked because you've learned my innermost thoughts.

I mustn't write anymore I have already said too much.

Because I love you,
Maggathie

December 6, 1967

My Dearest Dennis,

Have you given up trying to care for me? As I read your last letter, I saw some kind of love showing me that you really care. You have not failed me. But as I read on, I felt that you were falling away from me as if you walked out on me.

Why is it that in times of misfortune we seem to drift apart rather than becoming closer to one another? Perhaps it is my fault. Have I ever given you happiness? No, only a love that might not mean much to you via air mail, only problems and heartaches that you can share and worry about without the satisfaction of feeling that you've helped me, and perhaps a silly blue octopus named Benjie.

I can only hope to explain how I intended my humble offerings to bring you happiness.

First of all I want you to know that Benjamen Leonardo Auggie is a very good friend of mine. He's sort of been that substitute for a shoulder to cry on. When I gave him to you, I hoped that the two of you together might do a better job of picking me up to my feet again.

You have helped me so much, Dennis. You have listened to me. You have advised and consented. You have hoped for me. This alone is far more than I ever expected. You haven't been here physically, but you, wonderful you, gave me the warmth of an embrace from away across an ocean.

My love for you is genuine. It has lasted through doubts and fears, unbearable heartaches, exciting romances and all via air mail.

I have crushed my feelings of impatience. I'm back to the way of giving you all that I can and freely accepting all that you can give without frustration, or anxiety. I am myself again.

Our last few letters have been strained, almost as if we bled the words. My only hope now is that there is still something left for you to give, still something left so that you can continue accepting my love.

As Always,
Maggathie

December 6, 1967

My Dearest Dennis,

I received another letter from you tonight. I am hanging between happiness and sadness. I am sad because you are depressed. I can only hope that my last two letters will lift away that feeling. You feel that you have failed me and you have not. I am happy because I have had an enlightenment. How foolish I was to have pushed you; to have asked you to commit yourself when you have already committed yourself without my asking.

I can wait until you can tell me face to face that you love me only if you really will mean all that it implies. I never want you to say those three words until they say all of what you said they would.

I can say them to you and I mean it. I haven't placed you on a throne, Dennis. I've only told you of what I have learned about you. My only disappointment in you could be that you cannot love me. If that happens, it will be difficult for me at first, but life will go on.

I am in a new social whirl right now. Everything is beginning to work out. My bills have stabilized to go along with my earnings; I have met many new acquaintances; my job is going along smoothly and you'll be home in four months.

I'm taking flying lessons. My first will be this Saturday and I must admit, I'm pretty shaky about a prop plane.

I received a letter of commendation from my boss equipped with a $25 raise. The letter will go on my record. (I am very proud.)

They have opened my grandmother's will. (They couldn't wait.) I have all of my mother's share of things. The building will be sold and I receive 1/5 of the profit of which I must give $500 to my brother and sister. She left me her wedding rings and claim to anything that I wanted in her apartment *providing that no one else wanted it. I felt very happy that she wanted to take care of me in this way, but I still don't think it's fair to my brother and sister. They belonged to my mother too.*

My dreams are still alive, Dennis. I hope you realize that. I don't think anything can stop them, unless you do.

I hope you don't regret that our relationship has gone this far. Even if it doesn't turn out, I pray that you won't regret whatever closeness we have now.

Please go on hoping, my Dennis, or else my dreams must die.

Love,
Maggathie

Around 7 December 1967

My Dear Miss Maggathie:

I am very sleepy now. It's 10:00 p.m., Thursday night, and it has not been a good week at all. We've been working about eleven hours a day since this week began and I think it's beginning to take its toll. Not difficult work, nothing back breaking or mind rending, just long hours, long, weary hours.

But I must write to you, Miss Maggathie, write and thank you. I had not been happy this week. I've been moping about the office, forcing smiles and feigning good cheer. Couldn't even help myself. Didn't know why I felt this way – just one of my moods, I guess. But then Thursday afternoon – a letter from you; a warm, beautiful letter.

You really do love me, don't you Miss Maggathie? Why? Why? Why? Shouldn't question. To question why you love me would be like a pauper questioning a gift of one million dollars. This is not the time for paupers to ask questions.

How I'm going to miss you this Christmas. A girl I've never dated; a girl I haven't been alone with for more than twenty minutes; and because of you, this Christmas will be my least joyous. Strange. Perhaps not so strange.

Cheryl and Henry have invited me over their home for dinner Christmas Eve; some consolation, but a very poor substitute. How I wish you could meet them. How I wish they could meet you. But they have met you already. They know you almost as well as I do. They must; they've heard me speak of you often enough.

I mailed your Christmas gift yesterday. Wrapped it at work. It's only a small gift, but about three of my friends helped me with the wrapping. They know what I feel for you and just had to share my joy. You may find the wrapping a bit weird and perhaps a bit childish, but it had to be something special.

Now I'm not even certain I'll be home in January. The Major's answers to recent proddings have not been as promising as I had hoped they would be. The nearest thing to a "yes" I can get is "I'll do my best." What frightens me is that his best may not be good enough. Too much depends on the unpredictable.

I am so tired. Please excuse me for not writing more.

Most Affectionately,
Dennis

CHAPTER 16

CHRISTMAS ISN'T CHRISTMAS

December 10, 1967

My Dearest Dennis,

It's one of those days again when I find it difficult to keep myself from writing to you. Today was not my day, just not my day. Nothing drastic just plain full of calamities.

At 9:30 A.M. I was awakened by an obscene phone call. At 2:30 P.M. I had my landlord and family up here for a spaghetti dinner. As I put the spaghetti into the bubbling water up to the top tiny little worms came a floating (no extra spaghetti -- no stores open). At 5:30 P.M. I decided to visit my sister Patsy, down came the rain as I stood petrified at the corner of Lyman and Haynes Court. It's only 8:00 pm -- what next, my love

(this letter sags).

My sister gave me a picture of you and now I have three. One (with the bird on your head) is taped to the leaf of my desk at work so I may gaze at it throughout the day. One is in my wallet to be carried wherever I go. This one shall be placed with mine on the stereo. Togetherness! (sigh). How handsome art thou!

I'm really trying to get that old Christmas spirit. Tomorrow I'll hang decorations and perhaps send out my cards. Most of what I have is home-made. I like them though. Next Monday I'll put up my genuine aluminum tree and probably will do my Christmas shopping (I'm not going all out this year). Songs like "Home for the Holidays," or "I'll be Home for Christmas," sort of crush everything, but the way I look at it is that Christmas will be late this year. December 25th will be everyone's Christmas, but mine won't come until January or March or April or May, is it? Are you coming home in January? (Silly question, if you knew you'd tell me) Right?

I must go now. (All out of writing paper). I wish you were here. I want you near me always. How I pray that my dreams will come true. I hope for your hopes and live for my dreams. Some life! Maybe someday...maybe someday you'll love me

as I love you,
Maggathie

Me at Trafalgar Square in London.

December 15, 1967

My Dearest Dennis,

I am very pressed for time. With this holiday season coming up, I now have two houses to prepare for Christmas, two sets of Christmas cards to write out, and two shopping lists to fill (my helpless father).

I'm very depressed because I have only a few minutes now (at work) to write and there is so much that I have to say to you. I promise I will make it all up to you.

My present will be your homecoming and I'm prepared to accept that belated gift. (You won't receive your present until I can hand it to you). Christmas is the day Dennis F. Depcik gets back to Chicago, not December 25th.

There is so much I wish to tell you, but my boss will murder me if he finds me writing when I'm supposed to be working.

I miss you.

Loving you,
Maggathie

After December 15, 1967

My Dearest Dennis,

I have some surprising news to tell you. First of all, I must have told you that I received a letter of commendation. Now I've received a $20 raise and a new part-time position. I am now a Gossard-Artemus model. I still have my regular job, but every Thursday I'll model and my salary will be $10 an hour. What I'll be doing is modeling originals that our designers have made. I can't hide my excitement. Clunky Maggie the model.

I do have my problems still. I have a new acquaintance known as the "Heckler." He calls constantly, usually to say things that aren't very nice and last night he waited for me to get to the top of my stairway and then yelled something very ugly. I pretended not to hear, but I'm very frightened. I know who it is -- a boy that I met, made a date with and then broke the date. I know of no way to put a stop to this without causing a scene. I'm prepared to kill if necessary, but I hope it never comes to a struggle. My father, my landlord and my friends have been alerted that I may need their help and so far I've managed to have full protection at all times. (I'm very glad I broke that date as I think the boy is actually sick.)

In spite of all the merry making going on it still doesn't seem like Christmas. Perhaps your being away has something to do with that. I wish so very much that you will be home soon. Without ever having you, I miss you.

I may go to New York for New Year's Eve. I don't have the money actually, but believe that I can scrape it up somehow. I love that place.

I must give you something very special for Christmas, but I still haven't thought of anything. It's easy to go out and pick up a tie or a sweater, but that's not my idea of a present. When I marry, *my husband will have it fairly easy shopping for me. For one thing, I like very personal gifts so he won't have to worry about sizes and then I don't expect expensive things. An engraved bracelet for $9.98 would mean more to me than a whole new wardrobe. A dozen roses for ground hog day, or hot dog day, or any day would mean more than a $50 gift certificate. I think I'm harder to please than most women. Most would think valuable things will satisfy them. I'm not so dumb. I want things that no one can ever take away from me - Things given from the heart not the pocket -- things that nobody else will ever get --- because nobody else will have someone feeling exactly the same about them. Can you understand that?*

Well, I must get to work now. Please write soon and be very careful. I'm worried about you.

Love,
Maggathie

December 18, 1967

My Dearest Dennis,

Tis the season to be jolly -- tra la la la la—la la la la!

Don't be discouraged
or full of the mopes!
Think of tomorrow –
and all of its hopes.

Don't force a smile
don't feign good cheer.
Tomorrow, my love,
will soon be here.

You must be strong
in all that you do,
because if you're sad
I'll feel that way too!

Let us be happy
although you're away
and make your homecoming
our Christmas day.

The End

Ain't I silly!-----??

Yes, I really do love you, Dennis -- and don't ask questions.

You're going to miss me this Christmas -- not nearly as much as I'll miss you. Oh, I have the weekend filled with things to do (office parties, family reunions, friendly get togethers, etc.), but I'll be empty inside because half of me will be missing -- you. (It's sounding as if we're married), but really, if you have ever studied Astrology (ahem) I am Cancer (the moon) and you are Leo (the sun) and the moon reflects the light of the sun. So, if you're not around, it will be a cold, dark Christmas. And you know, Christmas can't be cold and dark, so (whew) Dec. 25th can't be Christmas. (I'm babbling again). I love you!

Stop! My landlady just brought my mail to me (a package from you). I refuse to open it until Christmas!! Thank you for the present but let me save my "real" thank you for when I open it. (It rattles!) (It's lightweight) (It's small). I bet it's a tape!! No, maybe, maybe it's -- no -- perfume? a picture? a knick-knack? I'll go crazy!!!!!! No, I refuse to open it until Christmas.

Oh, Dennis, I feel so badly I didn't send your present. I wanted to give it to you in person. I doubt if you'll like it --- you may think it too personal -- oh well. Can you wait until you'll be home? Oh, I feel awful. I'll send it as soon as I can. Oh, please forgive me! Probably everyone sent you a present, and I – the one who claims to love you most – like a dope, I wanna wait! Oh boy!

Answer Time:

The picture Patsy gave to me is a wallet size picture of you in uniform (colored) similar to the one you sent (or did you) but you have a smile on your face in this one. Very nice! But I think all the pictures I have of you are discrediting to you.

You must be home in January. If you're not, I'll be tempted to come to see you!

I must go. Merry December 25th.

With deep love,
Maggathie

Picture of me that Maggie's sister gave her.

After 18 December 1967

My Dear Miss Maggathie:

What a beautiful letter I've just received from you. I hadn't been in the best of moods of late – not being home for Christmas and working ten to eleven hours a day hasn't exactly prompted me to shout for joy. But your letter, your beautiful letter has really cheered me up.

Thank you so much for your poem. "Ain't I silly." No, not in the least. I'm wild about your poem, Miss Maggathie.

"Let us be happy
Although you're away
And make your homecoming
Our Christmas day."

Thank you for that last stanza. Thank you for ending your letter by wishing me a Merry December 25th. Christmas doesn't come in December this year.

"Oh, Dennis, I feel so badly. I didn't send your present. I wanted to give it to you in person...Oh, I feel awful...Oh, please forgive me." Forgive you for what; for not giving a Christmas gift on December 25th when Christmas doesn't fall on that day this year? Forgive you for caring so much that you wanted to wait to give your gift in person? There is nothing to forgive. If you haven't already sent the gift, you needn't. I'm a very patient man and can wait for our Christmas.

I spoke with the Major again the other day about my chances for a trip home in January. He informed me that he had called Washington and learned that several couriers expressed an interest in spending a week in Europe next month. I won't know for certain what the chances are for at least two weeks, but if I do get an opportunity to come home, it won't be until after January 10th. All we can do is hope – seems as though there's been a hell of a lot of that lately.

Most Affectionately
Dennis

P.S. This is a terrible letter, but you must forgive me. I have been very tired of late and have not been able to devote the time I would like to write to you.

P.P.S. Out of curiosity. You should have received my tape by now. Do I sound warmer on tape than in letters?

I want so badly to go home—to be with Maggie. Yet, everything is out of my hands. Because we're down two couriers, I'm stuck here unless someone from the Washington Station is willing to spend a week in Heidelberg. God, I pray this happens. But if it doesn't, I may not get home until my discharge in April. What if Maggie won't wait that long?

Before Christmas 1967

My Dear Miss Maggathie:

I've been thinking about you today (like any other day), but suddenly I became a bit disturbed. You love me – and I can't begin to tell you how glad I am of this. You love me, and I sit here somewhat content – content that was until I began to think of something. You tell me that you love me and all I say to you is – I care a great deal for you. Suddenly I began to realize an alarming possibility: suppose my caring a great deal for you isn't enough. Suppose you tire of my imperceptible admissions and in course tire of me. Have patience with me, Miss Maggathie, I'm slow in giving myself completely.

Very Affectionately
Dennis

CHAPTER 17

CHRISTMAS IN JANUARY

December 25, 1967

My Dearest Dennis,

I have just returned from a family get-together (it's Dec. 25th) and I must write to the man who has been in my dreams and on my mind throughout the holiday festivities. I have never missed you more.

I must thank you for your beautiful gift. Not only is it an elegant piece of jewelry, but the sentimental value of it will increase each day as my love for you increases each day. It is truly the most precious of all my gifts because it came from you. I will always treasure it. I can tell that you did not simply "pick it up" in a hurry just to "buy me off" so to speak. You must have given this gift very much thought as I could not think of anything that would have pleased me more -- just the right personal touch.

One thing worries me. My grandmother always told me that pearls received from someone you love bring tears. Maybe now she will prevent those tears.

I played your tape ---- with difficulty. It seems your voice was muffled by loud music. My brother was able to muffle out the music with a piece of cellophane and all went well.

I am very thrilled with all that you <u>*said*</u> *to me. Some things you had already written to me, but hearing these things have made me realize how much I am missing you while you are away. What a difference, Den. I will be sending you a tape within the next two weeks.*

You mentioned how little you have given me. You have underestimated yourself again. Dennis, without you I have no hopes, no dreams, no future. I want you very much. You have given me a purpose more real than anything I have ever experienced. If you knew how you've affected <u>*my*</u> *life, you would understand how serious I am when I say all this. I will save further explanation to that for the tape.*

One thing you must realize is that it is not only true that I do love you, but also that I <u>*can*</u> *love you. This will be difficult to get across to you. Perhaps this too must wait until it can be "heard."*

My tape not only will explain or try to pinpoint the "why" of my feelings; it will also be a type of confession. There are so many details to my story that it would be a loss to write them all. At least if I can talk to you, you could hear the expressions in my voice. Reading my thoughts may only bring you doubts. I know it will be difficult for you to understand what I must tell you. I pray that you will.

I want you to realize too that I have not shut out the world for you. I have tried to forget you, tried loving others, but I cannot. It's not as if I'm depending on your love; it's not as if my world will end if you cannot love me. All I can say is that right here and now, I must love you. I cannot do anything else.

I am a woman now. Even I must admit that. I do have many childish ways, but I do realize what is expected of me as a woman and all that the word "woman" implies. All the grief, hardships and sacrifice that come with womanhood are not new to me. I've lived through some of them and can accept even more.

As for your coming home in January, I can only say that I am praying and hoping along with you.

You must believe that I'll never stop waiting for you. God knows that I won't. I have dated so many fine, eligible young men since my engagement was broken. That first date may set me wondering, but after knowing these men I find that my love is still directed toward only you. I have many wonderful times, but no relationship can proceed beyond that point. These men are <u>here</u> <u>now</u> to dry my tears, to move heavy furniture, to hold me near and yet although you are an ocean away, you have done so much more for me. Believe that, Dennis.

I must close now. I have work tomorrow and it's nearly midnight. Besides, if I keep on, I'll never be able to stop.

Loving you,
Maggathie

P.S. I missed you so much this past weekend.

December 26, 1967

My Dearest Dennis,

Have I told you how I spent the Christmas holiday? Friday, I went to a party that consisted of a certain crowd from work. It was my first office party and it almost shocked me to find how status is forgotten about. It was rewarding as well as a good old bash. I really enjoyed myself. Saturday, my father decided that I should do his Christmas shopping. Have you ever tried shopping on the Saturday before Christmas --- for a dozen people to boot!? Saturday night several couples got together and we wined and dined and danced until dawn. (I was exhausted). Sunday, I cooked a spaghetti dinner for my dad and later went caroling with my usual crowd and followed that with midnight mass. Monday, I went to my sister's and then to my brother's and then to my sister's again. Later I wrote to you. I forgot to mention that I also spent a few hours at your brother Tom's house on Sunday. My sister needed a lift there so my friend and I tagged along all the way. I was busy, I was jovial --- I was lonely, I was in love and missing someone very much --- you.

I have absolutely zero plans for this coming weekend. I hope I find some way to pass the time. I think I'll cry if I must spend the New Year holiday alone -- and yet, I'd rather do that then simply go out and have a miserable time with just anybody.

I could go to a party, but I'm not particularly fond of the crowd --- they'll drink until they're out of their minds. No, I think I'll stay home and dream at midnight on December 31st, 1967.

My Dennis, I must go. I have so much sleep to catch up on. I will write as soon as possible.

With Love,
Maggathie

P.S. I can't wait to begin counting the days until you are home. I've estimated it to be 112 --- however, I may be way off.

Around 31 December 1967

My Dear Miss Maggathie:

I am anxious to receive your tape. Your letter has placed an aura of mystery about it: "...it is not only true that I do love you, but also that I can love you. This...too must wait until it can be heard...My tape...will explain...the 'why' of my feelings, it will also be a type of confession...I know it will be difficult for you to understand what I must tell you. I pray that you will."

I had hoped that you had planned to send a tape back, but I didn't want to commit you to doing so. It's been over a year since I've last heard your voice and I've almost forgotten what it sounds like.

I'm very glad you liked your gift. I didn't quite know what to get you. At first I had thought of buying you something for your apartment, but then decided that somehow that wouldn't say anything – and the gift had to say something. I'm happy that you enjoyed it.

I talked to one of the couriers from Washington this week. He informed me that their Major has been asking if there are any couriers who wish to take a week leave in Europe during January. Several couriers were supposed to have expressed an interest, but nothing definite yet. I'm going to have Major Swift call Washington tomorrow (I mean Tuesday) to see what progress is being made.

I'm going to have to stop now, Maggathie. I have to check the office to see if there have been any telephone calls for the Duty Officer. I'll write to you again as soon as I am able.

Very Affectionately +
Dennis

P.S. I think it should be P.P.S. instead of P.S.S.

January 3, 1968

My Dearest Dennis,

I have just returned from a hectic weekend in New York. Very disappointing for a holiday weekend. This truly has been the worst of all New Year's Eves I have ever experienced.

At this moment I am very content. (Irony) I am beginning to realize that there is more to my love for you than I had known. I mustn't be another Scarlett O'Hara with her love for Ashley, so I won't explain that statement. I can say that I find that I cannot hide nor halt my love for you. I have tried in vain.

I won't be sending you a tape for some time. My recorder does not maintain a moderate speed, so unless you don't mind my sounding like a hypo one minute and a silly chipmunk the next, you must wait until I can find someone with a good recorder (German-made).

I've always considered myself an eternal shopper as if I had my own retail shop. I've always seemed to meet someone better than the one I'm with. This is not so with you. I'm waiting for you; waiting because if you should decide to take me, I shall never want to leave -- not ever.

Someday you'll feel this way about someone. I will be happy for you then, even if I am not the one wreathed in your love.

I must go now. I am so very tired. There is something about thought that sometimes makes you tired. I don't want to stop.

Loving You,
Maggathie

4 January 1968

My Dear Miss Maggathie:

My New Year's Eve was --- quiet. I accepted Jim and Frankie Cox's invitation to supper. We purchased a bottle of champagne and at the stroke of twelve, toasted to each other's health and happiness: An almost solemn manner of bidding a new year welcome.

I don't know exactly when I'll be home in April. My commitment to the Army ends April 14th, so I should be home before then. I've recently received a form to fill out which stated that I was scheduled to depart Europe on or about 6 April, but that word "about" could extend over a number of days.

I may have blown my trip home in January. Several graduate schools that I am applying to request that I take a Graduate Record Examination Aptitude Test. They implied that I take it as soon as possible, for my score must be considered before my application is accepted. The earliest date available in Heidelberg is 20 January. Therefore, if Washington arranges a trip back home for me which would prevent me from taking this test, I would have to refuse it. So, now not only does my trip home depend on unforeseeable circumstances, but I have added a foreseeable one which could conceivably destroy the only chance I get. Another new hope has been added: let's hope I get my trip home and that it does not fall on January 20th.

I drank a silent toast to you New Year's Eve. Raised my glass of champagne to an empty chair, gave an almost indiscernible nod, and drank. Maybe I'm beginning to crack.

Most Affectionately
Dennis

P.S. How serious were you when you said: "You must be home in January. If you're not, I'll be tempted to come and see you."?

January 7, 1968

My Dear, Sweet Dennis,

Hi! It's snowing heavily here in Chicago. There are news flashes of abandoned cars left on the Outer Drive. The wind howls through the gangway and I sit here warm, content, close to the one I love.

I have just finished washing my hair and I can't decide if I should cut it or not. It's not billowing to the floor, but is becoming difficult to manage and keep in a somewhat fashionable style. Perhaps an inch or two will come off.

I have so much housework to do! I've let the chores go weekend after weekend and now I must tackle everything at once. It's not that I'm living in filth, just mass confusion.

I haven't checked the mail so there may be a letter from you. I should've thought about that before I washed my hair, but knowing that I heard from you just two days ago makes the presence of a letter from you very improbable.

How I miss you, Dennis. My heart actually sputters when I think that maybe there is some chance for us. But I can't think about the future for very long as too many "ifs" and "buts" worry me. It's not my lack of confidence that troubles me, it's the possibility that if things don't work out, I'll have to go on looking for that special someone.

It would be wrong to say that I'm tired of looking. I'm far too young to be tired. Maybe I'm too impatient or full of anxiety. (Should I take tranquilizers?)

I'm beginning to wonder if I should save my confession until I can see you. Really, it isn't that drastic, but can put a different light on the way you feel about me. That's when I must add explanation. That's when I'd like you near me, so that you could not only hear me, but read every emotion in my eyes.

It just occurred to me that if you were home, we would probably never really get to know each other as well as we have through our letters. We'd be too busy having a good time or something. I don't want it to be like that, do you? Promise me that we'll always have time to learn about each other.

Boy, all my girlfriends are getting married within this next year! That's my life! -- first one engaged – last one married. I shouldn't let myself be troubled over it. I've had the offers, but I think I'm too fussy. My poor husband will have to be a saint or just as crazy as I am.

Loving you,
Maggathie

9 January 1968

My Dear Miss Maggathie:

I'm sitting here listening to Streisand ("Color Me Barbra") and thinking of you. She does that to me. You have spoken so much of listening to her and of projecting her songs into your life, that I can't help but associate her with you. In a way, you're with me tonight.

I have a question to ask you. It results from something I learned today. May I have the pleasure of your company the evening of 23 January? I'll be home for two and a half days.

It finally came through – all those hopes and prayers weren't wasted. Unless the courier who agreed to come to Europe becomes seriously ill or dies, I should be leaving Germany 22 January and arriving in Washington late that same day. I hope to catch a flight to Chicago the same day, if possible, or early the next. I must be back in Washington the 26th of January and will have to depart Chicago the evening of the 25th. It won't be much time, but it will be something. Eureka – there is a God.

I will have a couple other events on my agenda while home. I must go to both Loyola University and the University of Chicago for interviews for graduate school. I hope to accomplish both of these in one morning, so too much time shouldn't be wasted.

Then, of course, there's the family. But you can be there too – with me. I must be with you as often as possible. There's so much we must say to each other; so much we must yet learn; so much and in so few days. But, at least this time we will be together – and for longer than the time it takes to drive from the orphanage.

Christmas on January 23rd. I feel like a child again. I must be one – did you ever see a grown man running down a main street almost kicking his heels with joy? Christmas on January 23rd – our Christmas. How I long for it.

There's so much to do – the calendar – the spaghetti dinner – the piano – the Civic Center and only two and a half days. But, we'll do them – as many as we can. Then again, maybe not the Civic Center, or the piano (if it's still at your father's house) – they can wait until April. For this time, just a quiet evening or two at your apartment – talking and learning more about each other.

Most Affectionately
Dennis

I will call you when I arrive.

January 16, 1968

My Dearest Dennis,

If you knew how goofy I'm acting ever since I heard the good news of your trip home, you'd probably think twice before coming! I laugh out loud at nothing at all. Have you ever ridden on a crowded bus and started to laugh -- and you're the only one laughing? How 'bout playing Password – everyone really engrossed in it, but I'm way off somewhere and three times gave the word that others are trying to guess as a clue! Instead of greeting everyone with "Hi," I say "Guess what, Dennis is coming home!"

Oh, you must call me the minute you arrive! I feel that I'm not making any sense. How will I compose myself this coming week?

We really won't have much time together. Even the spaghetti dinner will be almost impossible as your mother has great meals planned for you. I'm sure you'll have to be home more than you thought. From the little that I've heard, I understand that your mother is very sentimental and will want you at home for most of your stay. Please don't be angry. I'd suggest that we forget about ourselves until April.

Perhaps I'm exaggerating the situation and I'll leave that up to you. Believe me, I want to be there <u>with you</u> as often as courtesy permits and if you should find a time when we can take off to seclusion, I'm all for it! But I felt I should warn you that the situation at your home is something that I've never coped with before and I'm leaving everything in your hands. Whatever you decide, I'll understand.

I wanted this so very much. To see you, be near you, hear your voice, and if it must be from across a crowded room, that will be enough. (I think)

I have the feeling that you may be disturbed with me at this point. Actually, I'm disturbed with myself. But we mustn't be disturbed. We'll be together and that's all that matters.

I have so many things to tell you. I'm sure we'll find some way of learning more about each other this week (I mean 2 ½ days).

You must call me the minute you arrive. I can arrange to have some time off from work. Of course, that's for you to decide. On the days that you'll be interviewing for graduate school, I'll be at work, but hope to take some time off so that we can be together as often as possible.

I'm so very excited I can hardly seem to control myself. I just had that strange feeling that you'd be home this month, that our hopes and prayers would not be wasted. Good grief, there is a God and how I love Him for answering my prayers.

There is so much you must learn about me. Sometimes I feel so tense when I think of all that I must tell you. I must confess that I'm counting very much on our relationship leading to happiness. It's sometimes frightening to place all your hopes and dreams on one slim possibility.

Dennis, I must end this or I'll be going on and on forever. This will be my last letter until I see you next week. How happy I am!

Take care in your travels. I want to write so much more, but now I can only wait for your call.

Loving you,
Maggathie

After 16 January 1968

My Dear Miss Maggathie:

I have nothing to say – but I must write. You have continuously been in my thoughts these past few days. Every song I hear, almost everything I see – reminds me of you. Last night I went to the movies and saw "Two for the Road" starring Audrey Hepburn and Albert Finney. I don't know why, I could hardly associate either myself or you with either of the characters, but I returned home with a burning desire to be with you.

I can't begin to tell you how much I anticipate our meeting. A year ago it would hardly have mattered if I saw you or not, now it means almost everything. I don't wish to frighten you by implying that these few hours could chart the future years, but I would be foolish to deny that possibility. We have so much to say to each other, so much to learn, and all in so little time.

I wish you could meet me at the airport, but I can't ask you to. The flight I am scheduled to arrive on doesn't depart Washington until 10:00 p.m., and then I'm not even certain if I'll be able to make that one. My flight from Germany should land in Washington about 6:30 p.m. I must then go to the Washington Courier Station to check in the material that I am bringing over. This might not be completed until 9:00 p.m. I must then hope to make the proper connections to get to the airport on time to make my flight. Yet, I do wish you could be there.

According to my schedule, I depart Washington at 10:00 p.m., 22 January and arrive in Chicago at 10:50 p.m. that same day. I will be on National Airlines flight 207. I haven't told my parents exactly when I'll be in for the same reason that prevents me from asking you to meet me – I'm not certain I'll be able to make that flight. In all probability, I should be able to, but, then again, complications could arise.

How I've longed for you this past week. Three days ago I reread all of your letters – fifty of them – with the hope of partially filling the emptiness I felt. Quite the opposite resulted.

Tell me, Miss Maggathie, how can a *vacuum* become any emptier.

I've become somewhat apprehensive about this confession you're saving for me, "Really, it isn't that drastic, but can put a different light on the way you feel about me. That's when I must add explanation..." I mustn't think too much about it though - my imagination is far too wild.

Another quote,

"It just occurred to me that if you were home, we would probably never really get to know each other as we have through our letters. We'd be too busy having a good time or something. I don't want it to be like that, do you?"

Answer: No. It isn't that way; it wouldn't have been that way; it won't be that way. If I was home and if we were dating, we would have really gotten to know each other. If there is one thing I love to do with a girl I am dating, it is talk. I would rather spend several hours sitting and talking than running about from one night spot to another. I must discover what a girl is, and I can only do this through quiet conversation. You'll see how much I enjoy talking next week.

Until I see you. (what a wonderful sound that has)

Most Affectionately
Dennis

CHAPTER 18

HOME AT LAST

I arrive in Chicago at 11 p.m. Monday (January 22, 1968) and will return to Washington D. C. early Thursday evening (January 25, 1968). I have family obligations and Maggie can only get off from work on Tuesday, so we won't have as much time together as we'd like.

***

Tuesday is our day to be alone: breakfast at IHOP, a quiet walk along the lake shore, lunch at a small Michigan Avenue restaurant, and grocery shopping to stock Maggie's cabinets.

That evening, after chocolate malts at Kunka's Pharmacy, Maggie and I relax in her apartment on Lock St. We sit on the living room floor talking and listening to several of our favorite albums: Streisand's *People* and *My Name Is Barbra* as well as *Fiddler on the Roof.* Maggie sits by my side, lying softly against me, her head on my shoulder and her legs curled beneath her. I hold her so close I can feel her body move with every breath.

As the quiet evening progresses, Maggie lifts her head off my shoulder, then places it back down, straightens her legs slightly, then curls them beneath her again. She sighs as if to say something, and then is silent. After repeating this several times, she whispers, "Dennis."

As I turn toward her, she slowly lifts her head from my shoulder, gently pushes herself from my side, and looking directly at me, haltingly says, "I, I need to—to talk to you about something."

My body tenses when I hear the slight hesitation in her voice and see the apprehensive look on her face. I don't think I'm going to like what she's about to tell me.

"I need to talk to you about the confession I mentioned in my letters."

I turn slightly from Maggie, trying to hide my concern and the nausea churning my stomach.

"Dennis, you need to look at me when I tell you this. You need to look at my eyes so you know I'm telling you the truth."

My heart pounds so loudly I'm surprised Maggie can't hear it. I know from our letters that this was going to come up sometime during my visit home. Maggie had said she would wait until she could tell me face-to-face. I'm not sure what to expect, but I'm sure I don't want to hear it.

I slowly turn my head toward Maggie and tell myself to stay calm and composed.

Maggie hesitates. "I'm so afraid to tell you this. I beg you to please listen and try to understand. Please believe I am telling the truth."

I steel myself and almost indifferently say, "Go ahead."

Maggie takes a deep breath, sighs heavily, looks down briefly then back up at me. She takes another deep breath and looks directly into my eyes. "About eight months ago … I met another guy."

My stomach flips. I turn my head and slowly look away. *Did she just tell me what I think she did? Be calm; don't get upset.* My whole body is getting warm and I'm hoping it isn't obvious to Maggie. My head is reeling; I can't move.

"Please listen, Dennis. Please wait until you hear everything."

After a few seconds, when I feel more in control, I slowly turn to Maggie. The thought keeps racing through my head. *She's telling me it's over.* My mouth is dry, my body's getting cold. I can't talk. I can't do anything but stare past her. I'm looking at Maggie's face, but I can't see her. Yet, every instinct in my body tells me to keep my feelings to myself. I don't want Maggie to know what this is doing to me.

"Dennis, look at me. You need to understand. It was a bad time for me. Nothing was going right. It seemed everybody and everything was against me. And you and I were just beginning to know each other. I met him; we dated quite a bit; and I thought I might be in love with him."

Finally, I blurt out, "Who is he?"

"You don't know him. He's in the Navy at Great Lakes Naval Base. He's from New York."

"New York!" Maggie's letters are flashing through my head. *All those trips to New York.*

The words stumble from my lips. "I'm not sure what you're trying to tell me. Did you love him? Do you love him?"

Maggie continues. "You need to know something else. You need to know he asked me to marry him and gave me an engagement ring."

I'm numb, but I quickly gather myself and calmly ask, "Did you take it?"

"Yes."

My body stiffens; I turn my head from Maggie and start to rise. Before I can lift myself further than a few inches, she grabs my arm and pulls me down next to her.

"Look at me, Dennis. I broke the engagement. He's a great guy, but I don't love him. I tried to fall in love with him, I really did, because I didn't have any hope for us—but I couldn't. I just couldn't. As long as there's some chance for us, I can't love someone else." Tears well in Maggie's eyes.

I'm still dazed and do all I can to remain calm and in control. "But, what about this guy?"

"It's over. It was over long before it ended."

I sit silently with my arms dead at my side and can't bring myself to hold Maggie. I can only stare forward in a haze. *How long has this been going on? How far did their relationship go? Is she telling me everything? What does she expect me to do?*

This train of questions comes to a jolting halt when Maggie wraps both arms around my left arm, slowly places her head back on my shoulder, and curls her legs beneath her. When I don't respond, she asks, "Dennis, are you okay? Please talk to me."

I sit in a trance, looking straight ahead. After a very long minute, which gives me time to gain control of myself, I turn to Maggie and calmly say, "Maggie, are you sure it's ended? I mean, I have no right to expect that you wouldn't be dating other guys. You told me you were; I just didn't know it had gotten so serious."

Maggie lifts her head and again stares into my eyes. "Dennis, please know it's over with him. You must believe me."

I can see in her eyes that she's telling the truth and somewhat confidently say, "I do. Honestly, I do."

We spend the rest of the evening listening to music, lightly touching on our plans for the following day, and briefly talking about a variety of insignificant topics—but there's an uneasiness between us. I'm still shaken by Maggie's confession but don't want to talk about it anymore. I'm not sure what to say and don't want her knowing how much this is affecting me. I told her in my last letter, "You'll see how much I enjoy talking next week," yet I can't say another word about the confession that's hit me so hard.

It's getting near midnight and I tell Maggie it's late; she has work the next morning and I have two appointments for graduate school interviews. We hug, briefly kiss, and the night ends.

Walking that long block home, I can't stop thinking about Maggie. Her words keep echoing in my head, "I met another guy…he asked me to marry him…gave me an engagement ring. It was over long before it ended… As long as there's some chance for us, I can't love someone else." Why did she feel she had to tell me this? She risked our entire relationship not knowing what my reaction would be. Yet she did tell me. How she must trust me. How she must love me. I should have grabbed her in my arms and told her how much I care for her and how happy I am she chose me. I should have kissed her and told her how I need her and want her to wait for me—I should have, but I didn't.

I'm still not sure where this relationship is heading. And I have to be certain.

CHAPTER 19

AFTERGLOW

26 January 1968

My Dear Miss Maggathie:

How I miss you Klunkie. What have you done to me? Fat chance I have of not making a mistake on my return flight to Germany. I can't count pieces; all I think of is this klunkie girl who almost falls when getting in or out of a car, who walks into people when trying to get around them, who makes a botched abortion of a college application. I can't watch material: all I see is this girl with an excited smile waiting at the airport, this girl hurrying home running down Lock Street, this girl, such a crazy girl, who makes me laugh hours after I've been with her. How can I listen to the instructions that will be given to me: all I hear is the soft sound of a piano followed by "Oh, I can't play; you make me too nervous." All I hear is the change in the tone of your voice when I called from Washington:

Me: "Hello."
You (Indifferent): "Hello."

Me: "Good morning, Klunkie."
You (Excited): "Oh, Hello!"

Klunkie, what have you done to me?

Maggathie, do you know how much I missed you Wednesday and Thursday when you were at work? You said you knew, but I find it difficult to believe that you could imagine how much I actually did. I couldn't stop thinking about you. Everything that happened the night before, almost everything you did and everything you said would be recalled to my mind. I'd be riding up the escalator at Marshall Field thinking of something you said and suddenly break into a subdued laugh. Or, I'd be walking down State street thinking of something you did and - bam - instant smile. You know, Miss Maggathie, you're good medicine for me: people need good medicine.

Maggathie, thank you for being crazy, for being klunkie, for being the girl you are in your letters. I wanted so badly for you to be as I hoped you were. So much depended on this meeting. For me, it was going to determine what our relationship would be. If things weren't as I had hoped, I intended to gradually loosen the bond which we had tied over the past year. Perhaps it wasn't right to place so much importance upon these three days, but I knew that what I learned then would definitely influence our relationship. And it has, Maggathie.

I want you to wait for me. I know I asked you before on my tape and I know you said you would, but I must say it again. I have never asked a girl to wait for me, but I must ask you. I don't know what this is that I feel for you now, but whatever it is I do know that it must be given a chance to be realized.

Maggathie, how I wanted you to come to the airport with me. I had to call you from there. When you didn't answer the phone, I was a bit disturbed; I couldn't imagine where you could have gone. In similar instances, I would have imagined the worse, but with you, I couldn't. For some reason I thought (or perhaps I should say – wanted to believe) that you were home, but refused to answer the phone. I had hoped that you wanted that day to be ours, uninterrupted by anyone else. When I called Friday and received your answer, I was happy.

I'm sorry that I must go now. I have to begin checking the material for my return flight to Germany.

Wanting You
Dennis

P.S. You do have pretty legs.
P.P.S. I don't think I'm scrawny.
P.P. P. S. How empty I feel.

Around 27 January 1968

My Dear Miss Maggathie:

I'm sitting in my apartment now listening to my album of "Fiddler on the Roof" and am convinced of two things: 1) that my album is far better than yours, and 2) that I miss you terribly. I never knew my room was so empty.

I've seen most of my friends since I've returned. You know what the first question was which they asked: "How was Maggathie?" You see, they all knew my main reason for going home. "How was Maggathie?" or "Did you get engaged?" or "When's the big day?" were salutations which greeted me. In a way, I was somewhat surprised that everyone (even some of the fellows that I don't number among my friends) knew about us. I guess I talk about you much more than I imagined.

I reread a few of your letters last night. I had to be with you in some way. I wish you were here.

God, I just thought of something. If you have such a difficult time getting into my parents Galaxy, what problems are you going to encounter with my Volkswagen? I guess I could have foam rubber running boards put on to save your ankles. What a klunk you are. I'm glad.

Maggathie, thank you for a wonderful Christmas. How happy I was those two and a half days. Perhaps I didn't show it enough and maybe I didn't say enough, but, honestly, I haven't felt as fulfilled in a long time. You've done something to me, Maggathie, something I'm still hesitant to admit.

You said several things our last night that were the cause of my getting angry. One was that I hadn't met your expectations and didn't do the little thoughtful things that you long for; the other was that if we were married, it probably wouldn't last two weeks; and the last was "I don't love you."

I think we spoke of the first one that same night, but let me speak of it again. You said that you thought I called you up Wednesday morning because I thought something was wrong Tuesday night when I left. You couldn't have been more mistaken. I called you up Wednesday morning because I missed you terribly. In fact, I wouldn't even have left Tuesday night if I thought something was wrong. I called you at work Thursday afternoon because I missed you terribly. I was at your apartment fifteen minutes before you came home Wednesday evening because I missed you terribly. I moped around downtown (not going for my interviews) and spent all Wednesday afternoon looking for a gift of the heart because I missed you terribly. I almost swallowed my supper whole Thursday night and raced to your house because I missed you terribly. I came to your apartment Tuesday morning without calling because I didn't want to wait that half hour you would have probably requested because I missed you terribly. You can only do so many "little things" in two and a half days.

You made a statement in reference to this which I would like to quote and then compare it with another quote of yours. When talking about these "little things" you said: "Just once, I would like to look at you and catch you looking at me. You never seem to be looking at me." The evening just before that when I was sitting in your kitchen chair and you were standing in the doorway of your front room you said: "Stop looking at me." You said it not with anger, but with pride. I don't know, perhaps you forgot about this. I'm just trying to rationalize the two statements. You see, Maggathie, the fact that you don't catch me glancing at you is not reason enough to conclude that therefore I am not. The truth is that I turn my head faster than you turn yours.

The other two statements almost go hand in hand and actually are closely related to the first one. The three statements came in about a three minute period: "you're not what I expected; a marriage between us wouldn't last two weeks; and I don't love you." How closely related these statements are and how frightening they can sound to a person who's just beginning to realize how much you mean to him.

Maggathie, it's getting late and this is my last sheet of paper, so I'm going to have to leave now.

Missing You
Dennis

P.S. Thank you for crying Thursday night.

29 January 1968

My Dear Miss Maggathie:

It has been a week since I last saw you and it all seems like a dream. I can at times find it difficult to really convince myself that I actually was home. It all seems so long ago.

I'm back in the old routine; same old apartment, same old faces, same old activities – only thing is, they're not the same. Nothing seems the same around here anymore. I miss you.

I set my expectations far too high today. I told myself that if you wrote me a letter Thursday and mailed it Friday, that perhaps I would receive it today. No such luck though – just a lousy check. I should receive it tomorrow.

How I long to hear from you.

Oh, I sent you a gift. I'm afraid I had to put a customs tag on it, so you'll probably know what it is before opening it.

It's getting late, Maggathie, and I must go. I knew I didn't have much to say or much time in which to say it, but I just had to be with you for awhile tonight.

Good Night Klunkie.
Dennis

January 26, 1968

My Dearest Dennis,

I've already written a letter to you, but I felt so lonely tonight that I disregarded the first letter so that I might fill the emptiness I feel by writing again tonight.

I keep straining to hear someone calling me "clunky." I don't even have anyone to be mad at me. You know, you really have to care for someone in order to be mad at them. I learned that last night -- among other things.

Oh for Pete's sake, I have to wait another two months to put up that calendar. One thing is certain, I don't need a calendar to keep track of the days until you'll be home once again. How I miss you, Dennis.

I finally washed the dishes from Monday and wiped up footprints from the kitchen floor.

I really shouldn't feel lonely. You're here with me right now. Not only because I'm writing to you, but you're here because I've washed my hair and there's no hair spray in it. You're here because if I play "Fiddler on the Roof" I will cry. You're here because when I run, I think I run like a girl. I really feel that I hardly miss you at all --- just when I'm clunky. Do I run like a clunky girl?

I'm not asking for anything, Dennis. Just a chance to know you better. Right now I'm sad, happy, frightened and challenged all at the same time. I'm sad because geographical distance makes it impossible to have you here with me; I'm frightened because of the need to have you feel that way about me, and I'm challenged because I have so much to learn. I'm sad because I'm happy and I'm happy because I'm sad. I'm frightened because I'm challenged and I'm challenged because I'm frightened. You'll understand that.

I think I need you, Dennis. I don't like opening car doors, or going to bed before midnight and I don't want to answer the phone anymore because I know it won't be someone simply asking me how I feel.

I feel very bad because I think that we hurt my father's feelings by not stopping to see him all the while you were home. It never occurred to me that he would feel this way and I can't imagine why! It is my fault. I didn't even call to talk to him since Monday evening. I went over to his house tonight after work and I saw the hurt all over him when he asked why we didn't stop in. I feel awful. I'll have to make it up to him somehow.

By the way, Christmas was wonderful just as I had hoped it would be. Thank you for making my Christmas wonderful.

I'm going to set my wooly locks so I can be my beautiful self tomorrow and then I'll sit in my bathtub (with water in it) and off to bed. I'm going right off to bed to fall asleep.

Thinking I love you,
Maggathie

January 31, 1968

My Dearest Dennis,

This will be a long and difficult to write letter. It will be a long letter because I have so much to tell you. I began letters Sunday and Monday, but my complicated, uncoordinated life wouldn't allow me to finish them. It will be a difficult letter to write because I have hair spray in my eyes.

Here I sit, heart bursting with joy, tears streaming down my cheeks, out-loud laughter echoing through the corners of my home and you ask – "what have I done to you!" I don't know what I've done to you, but whatever it is may it grow and last forever. I want that more than anything in this world (No exaggerating).

How I want you, Dennis. I have so much explaining to do that I'll have to control these outbursts of a thinking love.

"You hadn't met my expectations"

"You didn't do the thoughtful things I long for"

"Our marriage would last two weeks"

"I don't love you"

Ha Ha Ha! Did I say all that? What a spoiled brat I am. You didn't fall all over me and let me walk all over you -- that was all! You proved to me that you were a real man (some thing rare these days) and proved to me that you weren't kidding when you said that your love for a girl would always last. (That's a switch)

Actually, you threw me completely off guard. I was hurt by a new realization -- that true love doesn't grow on trees. In defense, I said things to heal my wounded pride, to show you that I could walk out on you at the whim of a moment, that I could make you see that I was not so foolish as to give my love when I was receiving nothing in return. What a liar I was and all because I was so blind. I couldn't even tell that you missed me, really missed me, and all because I didn't really know you.

And you don't know me. One correction I would like to make is that I said "Stop staring at me," not with pride - I said it with self-consciousness (my inferiority complex). And wondering why I didn't catch you looking at me made me wonder if you didn't look at me – was it because you didn't like what you would see. Now that I know your head moves faster than mine, I feel that I have nothing to be ashamed of (a disadvantage of being clunky). I'll have to practice moving my head fast.

As for our marriage lasting two weeks – well, that was the *classic. Here we hardly really know each other and I make a statement that juvenile.*

You asked me to wait for you and I know you meant it. You know the answer – I'll wait for as long as it takes to prove one thing; that we can be happy together for the rest of our lives.

One thing I must ask you. If there is ever a time when I don't seem to understand you, please give me the chance to try. Don't lose faith in me too quickly. Let me learn, for I feel that I love you and with that love, a need to have you always. I don't want to lose you because of something as stupid as stupidity.

I guess I do miss you after all. A strange feeling is in me and it's almost frightening --- You may be displeased by this next piece of news. First of all, I must tell you that what feeling I have for you now stems mostly from the three days we spent together and your last two letters. It's funny how sure I was of my feelings before you came home, and once you were home, so unsure at times, and now so sure again. I've changed so in a certain respect. When I'm with girlfriends and happen to catch a guy's eye, I couldn't care less. If the phone rings and I'm asked for a date, I'm either too busy or too tired. I'm still me, flattered to all ends, happy to get the attention, but still indifferent.

I know by asking me to wait for you, you didn't imply that I should sit around moping – being a true-blue Nelly. But I am anyway. Not for any other reason than that I can't do anything more. Oh believe me; I'm not making life miserable for those around me by pouting all day. I'm still happy go lucky and my usual happy to be alive self. The only difference is my purpose - you. I'm not putting up a front anymore, I'm really happy. <u>You're</u> making me feel this way so why "put on" for anyone else. I'm happy thinking I love you and there's not much more that anyone else could do for me to let me feel this happy.

I have a terrible feeling that everything I'm telling you is coming out wrong. I needn't worry. You'll question anything that you don't understand and I'll explain in my next letter.

I quit modeling forever! Boy, that phase of my life didn't last long. I just couldn't stand another dousing of that clown make-up and the sound of that one old bug purring the word "Yummy" every time I tried on something new.

Dennis, I hope you'll always feel a need to be near me. You know, not holding hands or rubbing legs beneath a table (well, that's not bad), but like what I feel for you -- to be able to look around to find you there, or call your name just to hear you answer. I need someone very much. That someone is you.

To think that the things that I worried about most --- being klunky, saying silly things, getting nervous, smiling too much --- are the things that seemed to please you most. I won't ever change for "anyone" and how wonderful to know that "anyone" doesn't want me to.

Has this letter made one bit of sense? I certainly hope so. I've tried to say so much, but I've found out that my point gets across faster when I'm speaking than when I'm writing.

I must go now. My eyes are crossing.

I think I love you, Dennis
Maggathie

P.S. You are a scrawn (155 lbs!!)
P.S.S. Thank you for the compliment on my legs.
P.S.S.S. You're welcome --- but I cried because I had to, not because I wanted to - so I don't deserve a thank you.
P.S.S.S.S. I know – it's supposed to be P.S
P.P.S.
P.P.P.S
P.P.P.P.S.
P.P.P.P.P.S.

I like clunky spelled with a "c" but it does give it a clunkier affect when one spells it with a "k." What's more effective?

KLUNK
or
CLUNK

P.P.P.P.P.P.S. I shouldn't have used affect in the last paragraph. Right, it should be effect?

(This letter needs to exercise)

CHAPTER 20

MAN AND WOMAN

February 1, 1968

My Dearest Dennis,

I had so much to tell you that I couldn't say everything in yesterday's letter. Now I can't think of a thing to tell you. How about if I tell you all about myself.

First of all, I'm a clunk and you know that. I'm crazy and you know that. I'm in love with you and you know that. What's there to tell you?

I miss you so very much. I get so tickly inside when I remember that you'll be home for good in about 60 days. I don't want to count on too much. I know you wanted to be home with me on your last three days, but I'm afraid that this need may lessen once you're home to stay. How I hope not -- pray not.

I'm writing as if in desperation for your homecoming. With all this trouble in Korea, Viet

Nam, etc. and then all the doubts of the future, I am filled with more anxiety than ever before.

I don't know why I worry so about what will come. It's silly to worry about things you can't really prevent. I guess when you need someone as much as I need you; you worry about things like that. When you've waited for someone whom you can really love, and he finally walks into your life, it's difficult not to worry about losing him. I won't bother you with this worry. I'm sure everything will work out for the best. Trouble is, what's the best?

I had a nightmare last night and funny – I can't remember what it was about. I woke up in the middle of the night petrified about something, but can't remember what! It was storming so maybe the thunder and lightening had something to do with it.

I miss you so much. Don't you hope things work out for us?

Everyone knew today when I got to work that I got a letter from you last night. They could all tell by the way I tripped over the extension cord of the kellogg phone, spilled a cup of coffee, dribbled pineapple jelly on my plum mini dress and (get ready) got my ankle stuck in between the back and the seat of my chair. Try that in a mini skirt with 6 people trying to get you out. They finally ended up suspending me in mid-air and turning the chair sideways.

I must go now. I will write again this weekend. I need you so much.

Thinking I love you,
Maggathie

P.S. I do

I wish you were here.

Around 7 February 1968

My Dear Miss Maggathie:

What must you be thinking by now? Three letters in the period of a week, then silent so long. It' isn't my fault though. The tremors caused by the Korean crisis had their effect upon our small station. I've been hopping about quite a bit in the past week. I even have little time to write you now.

I'm very sorry we hurt your father's feelings. The idea that he might be offended at our not stopping to see him just never entered my mind. There were so many things that had to be accomplished in those two and a half days. Too many things in too short a time. I'm really sorry.

Actually, I shouldn't be writing to you now. I'm in one of my moods again tonight. It suddenly hit me toward the end of the work day. No real reason: suddenly, I was in a depressed mood. It's really at times like this that I wish you were near. Why – if I was home, I'd just drag myself over to your apartment; sullenly knock on your door – and talk, that's all, just talk. I wonder if you can tolerate my moods and how you will react to them.

"You didn't fall all over me and let me walk all over you --- that was all!" I'm somewhat surprised that you might have expected anything else. I believe in a very definite relationship between man and woman. The man must be the master, a benevolent and understanding master. He must be the one who does the leading – not one who follows. (Would you believe that few things anger me more than to go shopping with a girl and have her dragging me behind her through the various department stores). Both the man and the woman must understand their roles and each must act in accordance with it.

Forgive me if I have belabored what may have already been an obvious point, but I had to make it as clear as I possibly could. I want you to understand my concept of a man and woman relationship. If you are still confused as to what my concept is, I wish you would ask me some questions about it.

“I won’t ever change for ‘anyone’ and how wonderful to know that that ‘anyone’ doesn’t want me to.” You know, Miss Maggathie, what you have said there is beautiful. Thank you so much.

No, Maggathie, I don’t want you to change. I don’t want to make you into anything other than what you are, because it is what you are that differentiates you from ...

(The letter ends here, as the rest of the pages are missing.)

February 8, 1968

My Dearest Dennis,

I must ask you to forgive me for not writing sooner. You must believe that I have at least three letters started to you and one completely written (from Saturday) that I never got around to mailing.

The past two weeks have been hectic. I've started at 8:00 a.m. every day at work and have worked as late as 8:00 p.m. I've really been running ragged. I also have some rather complex problems to solve, and decision making after long meditation can tire me easily.

All and all I should have at least found time to let you know that I hadn't forgotten you. Believe me, I didn't. You played a major role in my meditation.

This has been a bad past two weeks for me like before when everything went wrong -- maybe now I have different problems, a different outlook, but it has that same haunting feeling. It's like graduating from big problems to even worse problems. Do I sound like I'm pitying myself again?

I finally did it! I finally fell down my stairway. Usually when the steps are slippery, I slide but save myself by grabbing onto a snowy banister (of course I don't have gloves on). But this time the klunk wasn't fast enough (as usual) and made it half way down the stairs without even trying (I had gloves on too!)

How can I explain to you that I miss you so very much? You'd think this feeling would fade with time. It only grows.

When I heard that Johnson may call up the reserves and extend enlistees, I nearly cried. I need you, Dennis, and they just can't do that to me. They just can't!

Pretty soon you'll be home again and that pretty soon means exactly just about 60 days! That's only about eight weeks, which means only two months and ads up to the same as 1/6 of a year, which in turn is 1,440 hours, or 86,400 minutes or 5,184,000 seconds! --- 60 days. In other words neither of us need hold our breath.

But how I miss you! I hope so much that everything works out for the best. Trouble is (once again) that best may not be realized for many moons. It's all in the stars?

Good night, scrawny,
Maggathie

P.S. I'm writing a book about myself, but I can't pick out a title. How about:
"How To Be Successful In Hairspraying Without Even Crying" or
"The Big, The Mad, And The Klunkie" or
"Bigfoot In The Park" how about
"Who's Afraid of the Holes Underneath the Sidewalk"

February 12, 1968

My Dearest Dennis,

I was sleeping so soundly, the third good rest I've had since I saw you. Then, a knock at my door startled me. The first thing that entered my mind was perhaps the mailman had a package for me or the gas company wanting to check my heater. But lo and behold --- it was a Jehovah Witness who talked about persecution for 15 minutes. Boy was I crabby. She finally left and I nearly cried until she yelled -- you've got mail -- a letter from you. And now I'm singing and very wide awake.

Gee, I wonder how I will react to your moods. First of all, I don't know you, so I don't know what could get you <u>into</u> a mood, or I don't even know if you'd want to get <u>out</u> of a mood! Don't tell me what to do though. Let me figure you out. Only you'll have to have patience with me, because I'm sure to flub up the first couple of times. Usually when I'm faced with a person who is moody, I'll just listen to their beef and combat the mood just by letting them know I care. Sometimes, I'll ignore a mood, act my casual crazy self, and (snap) I've got a smile out of them. Sometimes, if they really ignore my attempts to help (boom) I'm in a depressed mood and we end up helping each other. Just give me time, if I haven't hit what could get you out of a mood, I'll figure something out.

The relationship between a man and a woman:

Yes, the man <u>is</u> the leader. This I believe with all my heart. Leadership is the biggest factor I look for in a man. I've found some that I could string along endlessly. What happens? I lose respect for them and all feelings other than pity. I've found some who were leaders (they thought), tyrants (I thought). If it's one thing I can't stand is a man who must constantly prove to me and to himself that he's a man. I know what a man is! You know, the *extremist who believes woman is the ground on which a man walks. And that's not a man at all! I've also found those with just the right touch of leadership, but something else is usually missing and (poof) all is lost. So you see, I'm fussy too -- sometimes too much so.*

One thing really disappointed me about you; the idea of shopping with a girl. I'm not talking about groceries or buying clothes for myself, but I get the biggest kick out of Christmas shopping with a man. I can recall Christmas' that shopping started a month in advance --- stopping for hot chocolate -- watching kids go up on Santa's knee -- looking at fancy window displays -- selecting just the right gift for just the right person. There's a great feeling there when two people who care about each other pick out a gift together for a person they <u>*both*</u> *care for. These past two Christmas' of shopping alone were terrible -- get* <u>*anything*</u> *and get* <u>*home*</u>*. Sorry, but that's the way I feel. A man who would toss the money at me to do the shopping for gifts is not the type to make an ideal relationship with me. I'm much too sentimental for that kind of thing. You're probably saying "Oh, humbug!" Sorry!*

Yes, there's a definite line between woman's work and a man's work. I honestly (with passion even) would not want to see my husband doing my work, especially dishes -- ugh, that disgusts me. For one thing, I wouldn't have much respect for him and I'm the type that I hate anyone to interfere with my housework and the way I do things. A suggestion? -- I'll listen. An offer to take garbage out? -- Fine and thank you -- Wash the floor because I'm in my ninth month of pregnancy? -- I love you. But that's it, kid!!! (Boy, I <u>*am*</u> *fussy!!)*

I do think a woman is a servant in certain aspects. A woman was made to please the man she loves. When a woman loves a man (speaking for myself) she should be a servant to him. A woman must be versatile. She has to be first of all a wife --

cooking, keeping house, managing the things her husband puts in her care. She must be a mistress. Someone dressed nicely to greet her husband when he comes home, never refusing his passion. She must be a nurse. Sympathetic and helpful when her man isn't feeling well. She must be a friend -- friendship in the true sense of the word must never be lost. Although certain things are a man's worry alone, a man still needs someone to turn to as a friend -- someone there to stand by him right or wrong. In time, she may be a mother too. The only comment I have on that (as I don't really know how it is to be a mother) is that the man in her life must never be neglected because of children and that's saying countless things.

Everyone that has heard these ideas of mine says --- ha, ha, ha, wait kid. You'll see! But, honest, Den, I've got certain ideals set up for the kind of wife I'll be. I've seen so many women make a beautiful relationship turn into a ploddy day by day, bogged down type of thing and I don't want that. Just because two people get married that doesn't mean they must turn into the typical statistical magazine analyzed way of life that I so often hear or read about -- does it? I won't get married if that's true!

I still haven't received your gift and curiosity has the best of me. One thing is certain --- I'll be pleased with it even if it was a souvenir napkin from a German root beer stand.

Missing You,
Klunkie

P.S. I pulled another one at work last Thursday. It was 5:00 and I emptied my ash tray into the trash can as I usually do, got all the way to the elevator and someone shouted -- Fire! So, we all rushed back, the office was filled with smoke and it would be my trash can that was burning! I got hell, but I told them I'd try harder next time. Now it's a big joke so all is well again.

P.S.S. Sears Roebuck is replacing my gas heater -- of all things -- it's leaking carbon dioxide!!

P.S.S.S. Sorry that this letter is such a mess. You'll probably have trouble making sense out of it as my punctuation is way under par.

Before 15 February 1968

My Dear Miss Maggathie:

It is Thursday afternoon and I am sitting in my living room listening to my stereo. I have just returned from having two wisdom teeth removed and decided to hasten a letter off to you before the Novocain wears off.

I received a letter from you - another long revealing letter. I'm afraid you have misunderstood me. Not your fault though, I certainly didn't make myself clear. It's about my not liking to go shopping with a girl. You seem to have interpreted my statement wrongly. I never said that I don't like to go shopping with a girl; I merely said that I don't like to be dragged about from store to store. And I mean just that – "dragged about." I don't like for the girl to be running from department to department, pulling me behind her like a little puppy or reticent child.

In fact, I really enjoy going shopping with a girl for whom I care. I have done it often in the past and will do it often in the future.

The bustle of downtown seems so much less frustrating when there is someone you can laugh with. And your memories of Christmas shopping aren't too far removed from mine. I enjoy few things more than standing with my girl in front of Marshall Field's or Carson P_ _ _ Scott's window display, shoulders hunched, hands in pocket, with my girl huddled next to me, hands wrapped around my arm, face close against me – looking and smiling. And watching the children, half dazed with wonderment at the gaudy displays. And who cares if you run half a block to catch a bus only to have the doors close when you are within three feet. How can you get angry when two of you are standing there panting with exhaustion.

As for "A man who would toss the money at me to do the shopping for gifts" – all I can say is "NOT I MAM." Perhaps you don't realize how sentimental I am. Buying a gift for someone special is not a casual event. No, Miss Maggathie, there will never be any "Here's $50, pick up some gifts for me." Any gift given as a joint gift will be jointly purchased.

You know, Klunkie, the more I learn about you, the less I wonder. So, your friends laugh and tell you to wait and see when you speak of being a wife, mistress, nurse and friend to your husband. Actually, all they are doing is admitting one of two things: either they have failed to be these to their husband, or their husband has failed to accept them as such. Either way, their laughter is rather derogatory to themselves.

"Just because two people get married that doesn't mean they must turn into the typical, statistical, magazine, analyzed way of life that I so often read or hear about --- does it?" Not if both feel the same way and work at avoiding it. You see, I think that kind of life can sneak up on you and if you're not careful – BAM – Ho, Hum – another typical marriage. And that's something I want to avoid at all costs. I think I know some of the symptoms and when I recognize them – immediate reaction.

The real work begins after you say "I do." Keeping the other person from wondering why he or she married you can at times be a difficult task. But, if both members are trying to accomplish the same, it can be a great deal easier. In short, with my wife's cooperation, I expect our marriage to be a growing experience of love. I want her to always be aware of why she married me. When she begins to ask herself "why," and can't find a satisfactory answer, then I worry – hopefully, before then.

A quote from your next to last letter: "How can I explain to you that I miss you so very much? You'd think this feeling would fade with time." No – I wouldn't.

Sorely Missing You
Dennis

February 15, 1968

My Dearest Dennis,

So, you got two wisdom teeth pulled. Well, you didn't need them anyway. I hope you didn't go through too much pain.

*I kinda figured you really liked to shop with a girl and meant "*being dragged*" to be taken literally. Any guy who would spend an afternoon searching for a gift -- a book of poems no less -- isn't the type to throw $50 at a woman and tell her to buy gifts. I just wanted to see if my hunch was right -- and it was.*

I miss ya, scrawn. I can't help feeling rather lonely all the time, But somehow, you're still with me.

It's 1:00 A.M. I worked until 8:30 pm tonight. Hey, I'm really running crazy at work. You'd think I was a courier or something. My duties today started off with taking minutes at a 3 ½ hour meeting. (That was fun -- especially when everyone talked at once). Then I was sent to Fields to buy a Werner girdle! (We're copy cats). At 3:30 I drove my boss to the airport (his car), drove all the way back to his house to pick up his wife and she drove me back to work. I can't figure why he just didn't leave the car home to begin with!

*What did you mean -- "*The more I learn about you, the less I wonder*"??? That I'm not mysterious? Don't answer that if you don't want to. I'm rather slow at picking up things. By the way, it's not only my girlfriends who laugh; my sister, my sister-in-law, and quite a few of the old timers smirked at my ideals. It's funny, my grandmother never laughed; she instilled these ideals in me. That was a woman. They don't make them like her too often nowadays.*

Your parents really are looking for a new home. And Patsy and Leo may have found "the" house. Gee, Bridgeport will certainly be lonely then. It frightens me to think that you may not be near me after all. What am I talking about; you may not even want to be either. Oh, I hope so.

So, I'm the leading lady in your plan. Well, buster, this young starlet better get some sleep or Frankenstein may want to take me for his bride.

Love,
Maggathie

P.S. Tell Benjie that he better stand up straight or he'll grow that way. I miss him too.

February 19, 1968

My Dearest Dennis,

It has been over a week since I last heard from you. How my heart worries as I feel you may be beginning that gradual break that you once mentioned. I only pray that this silence only means that you've been busy, or much too exhausted to write.

I must tell you that I wore the bracelet and the pin that you gave me, and I was flooded with compliments, followed by ohs and ahs wherever I went. How proud I was in telling everyone that they were gifts from you. I am very thankful for them and you.

I miss you, Den. And I'm so worried because I haven't heard from you. Are you making a fool of me this time? Do it quickly -- if you must do it at all.

I must be off. I will write more later this week. I guess I'm just running away – afraid.

With love,
Maggathie

CHAPTER 21

SELFISH REASONS

Around 19 February 1968

My Dear Miss Maggathie:

Let me tell you something I was going to leave unmentioned. When I returned to Germany from the States, I was approached by the Major who very excitedly said, "I want you to think about extending. I've just found out that all you need do is extend for one month and you can make Captain." I thought about it for two days. The advantages: 1) more prestige, 2) about $400 more than I would have if I stayed in an extra month as a first lieutenant, and 3) an opportunity to see more of Europe. The disadvantages: another month away from Miss Maggathie. You should have seen the look on the Major's face when I declined.

Klunkie, Chicago holds little of interest for me. If it wasn't for the fact that you were back home waiting for me, I would have certainly stayed at least the extra month. "European out" and spend the summer touring Europe. This opportunity is here

– now. But you are in Chicago. A simple choice of what I want most. I'll be home in April.

I can understand why you may have felt as you did. I have not had much free time to write, and you being you, naturally assumed the worst. I just want you to know that this is not so. A person who hungers for your letters as much as I do could hardly be starting "that gradual break."

You know what I really miss, Klunkie? - Waking you up in the morning. Pretty silly isn't it.

I really miss you.

Most Affectionately
Dennis

P.S. I think we'll hang our calendar in your bedroom.

Around February 22, 1968

My Dearest Dennis,

I feel that I must rush this letter off to you, not only because I have neglected you, but also that there is so much that I must say to you.

The letter I received from you today made me float onto cloud 9. I can't believe that this is happening to me. It's almost as if someone said, "Maggathie, you are by far the best woman on earth" (the speaker being someone who really knows what he's talking about).

Which brings me to the subject of --- Are you sure you knew what you were doing when you refused a one month extension. Den, am I worth all that? Believe me, I want <u>you</u> home near me as soon as possible, but I don't want you making the sacrifices for <u>my</u> selfish reasons. I won't be hurt if you think it over and decide to stay, but I will be hurt if you come home in April and end up regretting it for the rest of your life. What if you don't like me anymore? What if suddenly you take one long look and find that I'm not that Maggathie you so often spoke of. Think it over, scrawn.

As for my neglecting you. Yes, I'm a terrible fink. I could give a list of excuses for letting moments pass when I could've written, but I'm afraid my No. 1 excuse is that I was afraid to write. I was almost certain your feelings had turned away from me. I'm stupid and so damn insecure!

So, Chicago holds little interest for you. Well, you know what, I'm getting fairly tired of it myself. I'm so worried about this "Long Hot Summer" that lies ahead, I'm tired of nosey neighbors who think that neighbors are people to be spied on and gossiped about, I'm sick of dirt and grit, and murder, and guys with fast cars, and Mrs. Whatchamacallit's fur coat, and empty stores, and you know what? I'm gonna find all that no matter where I go. What's a Klunk like me to do?

Hang our calendar in my bedroom? I have a pink bedroom, scrawn, how's a gold calendar with red knobs gonna look in a pink bedroom – (silly). I guess your idea has its advantages --- like - all I have to do is ask you for the date and I've got you trapped – or when I wake up I'll think of you because it's sure to catch my eye -- and it might even cover that spot that I forgot to paint.

I haven't pulled any smashing Klunk-type things since I nearly started Gossard on fire, but I've been exactly 3 minutes late for work for the past two weeks, I sent a very important letter to Skokie, Illinois via air mail and it took an extra two days to get there, I threw an ice cream cone out of an unopened window – cone and all slid so gracefully down the side of my bosses car, I left my keys in my door for nearly 24 hours, and washed my dad's navy blue shirt in bleach. Boy, I'm so dumb. Actually, I do have a head on my shoulders when needed, otherwise I forget about it.

I'm enclosing a picture that I modeled for. I must admit that it doesn't look at all like me. (I think I'm cuter than that, don't you?) By the way, we weren't really in Dallas, I'm not really his secretary, and the office I work in isn't nearly as plush.

Your Valentine was very beautiful, your Happy Sunday after Valentine's Day card knocked me off my feet and that card with the octopus on it made me miss Benjie (Our Benjie) (sigh). If only I could be there to see him now --- growing, growing away from me (sigh). Does he still have his eyes?

I miss you, scrawn. You know if you were home I'd be a million times more content and happy. I could cuddle you, and run away from you, and wrestle with you, and laugh with you, and cry with you, and talk with you, and be quiet with you, and walk with you, and ride with you, and work with you, and go to the zoo with you, and shop with you, and sing with you, and eat with you, and (getting monotonous????) sleep with you (Ah Ha, getting better eh!), and fight with you, (for variety only) and love with you, and on and on and on.

But I must run off now. I'm baby-sitting for Patsy and Leo tonight and I've discovered that I have about five minutes to get there only 10 minutes late.

Loving You,
Maggathie

It's been a month since I've been with Maggie and I'm missing her more with each letter I receive. I reread "I miss you scrawn…and on and on and on" over and over again. I don't know how I'm going to last another six weeks in Europe. She's on my mind constantly.

It's a sunny Saturday afternoon, and while casually strolling the streets of downtown Heidelberg, I come across a small sweet shop with a window displaying a variety of stuffed animals and assorted candies. I glance inside as I pass. After only a few steps, I find myself back at the window. My eyes are drawn to the stuffed animals where there sits a little black cat with flowers on its head. I'm not a cat lover, nor do I think is Maggie, so I pay little attention to it as I enter the shop to see if I can find a stuffed animal or something else Maggie might like. I'm not looking for anything expensive, just a little gift from my heart—something that whispers "Maggie" to me. After about a half-hour of squeezing almost every toy animal in the store and not liking any of them, I find what I want: a frosted crystal statue of the Blessed Mother and Child.

As I leave the small shop, Blessed Mother and Child wrapped in paper and resting safely in a gift bag, I'm drawn again to the window display. That damn black cat with flowers on its head catches my eyes again and I soon find myself back inside asking the clerk to wrap it up.

The following Monday, I mail my gifts to Maggie with an enclosed note to explain the one that is not so obvious.

Around 24 February 1968

Dear Klunkie:

I would like you to meet "Mestopholis" – "Mes" for short. He was sitting in the window of this sweet shop downtown and began to whimper as I passed. Quite naturally I couldn't believe my ears and continued on my way – the whimper progressed to a whine. Well, now a whine does something to me that's difficult to explain. I stopped and turned – goodbye heart.

"Mes" has this tremendous yearning to go to the States – Chicago of all places. Quite naturally I began to tell him all about you. What a sad mistake that was. I'm afraid I've lost him to you. He tried to break it to me gently – something about boy/girl relationship. I cried a little.

I made him promise one thing though – that he would put those flowers in his hair and disguise himself as a female. You see, I can't take the chance that he'll steal <u>your</u> heart from <u>me</u>. Damn Cat!

Most Affectionately
Dennis

Around February 27, 1968

My Dearest Dennis,

I'm writing on Theresa's Big Scribbler Tablet and as you may guess I'm baby sitting again for Leo and Patsy. (They're <u>still</u> searching for a house)

What am I talking about? I received your presents and I can't get over how really great that statue is. I was at first worried that it might glow in the dark. I could just see me waking up in the middle of the night to find something glowing in the corner of my room! But really, Den, the Blessed Mother and I are very close. Actually, we've been under a special bond since about 1961, not only because she's my patron saint, but more because she really has taken good care of me since the absence of my own mother. You don't know what it is to miss a mother, so you really can't imagine what comfort having The Blessed Mother trying to replace my mother brings to me.

Well, "Mes" is really a heart warmer! The flowers fooled me for awhile, but this old Klunk ain't so stupid after all. "Mes" confessed that Chicago and I would be more enjoyable if you were here (I think so too). By the way, did "Mes" meet Benjie?

Oh, how I miss you.

I was just looking at "Mes" and he has the fattest tail! (And very scrawny legs!) Oh, well --- "Mes" the Greek with scrawny legs and a fat tail. Somehow those flowers do "something" for him (oops, I hope he doesn't see this). I wouldn't want him to think that I'm not the Maggathie that you told him I was.

It really snowed today in Chicago. I was rather angry at that old snow! I was hoping I could toss my boots and begin shopping for dresses in pinks and blues again. But no, just when I think spring is on its way, just when I think April is only a skip and a jump away --- Boom --- snow!! I like snow alright but not when I've already dreamed about spring.

I really hope everything works out for us, don't you? I don't know what plans I fit into in regards to your future. You may ask me to wait for three more years, or maybe you'll say "run away with me now." Whatever the future holds, I hope that it will work out for the best for both of us.

One thing I'm wondering. Do you feel that you know me now -- at least better than before you were home? I'm really very easy to figure out. Right?

Oh, I suddenly don't feel too well. I keep getting chills and my throat is very sore. Gee, if I'm coming down with something, I hope that I haven't passed it on to the kids.

I'm getting awfully sleepy. I think I'm going to lie across Pat's bed and see if I can catch up on some rest.

Forgive me for leaving you hanging like this. I'll write again as soon as possible, okay? OK

Loving You,
Maggathie

P.S. Mes says "Meee (Good night) Ooowwww

I hope there aren't any germs on this letter.

P.S.S. "Mes" looks like a boy cat with flowers in his hair.
P.S.S.S. Mes must be Greek – he walks backwards.
P.S.S.S.S. Do you swallow your gum?

Late February 1968

My Dear Miss Maggathie:

I'm terribly lonely tonight. The day at work had not been a good one at all. Even your letter didn't help. In fact, it was more your letter than anything else which has made me feel this way. I felt so close to you when reading it, that it made your absence so much more felt. I want to be with you.

Which brings me to the subject "...I want you home, near me, as soon as possible, but I don't want you making the sacrifices for my selfish reasons." Correction, Miss Maggathie, I am not "making the sacrifices for your selfish reasons," but rather, I have made the decision for my selfish reasons: I want to be home with you as soon as I possibly can. I had a choice to stay an extra month in the Army and acquire some prestige and quite a bit extra money, or to come home to you a month sooner. It wasn't really much of a decision: I simply chose what meant far more to me.

God – I could never be a bachelor my entire life. I simply couldn't take too many evenings like this one. I'm alone and for the first time in quite awhile, I'm aware of it. I do enjoy being alone though. I enjoy being alone with a girl also, not solely for the reasons that you're thinking of, Klunkie. I mean, just sitting and talking with each other, or just sitting and being with each other.

I was talking to a couple of German acquaintances last night (girlfriend and boyfriend) and they brought up an idea which fascinated me and I would like your reaction. They thought that after a couple had been married for awhile, they should have separate bedrooms. They reasoned that this would have numerous advantages: the husband would be spared the sight of his wife greased down and pinned up; the wife would be spared the discomfort of a snoring husband; both would have a great deal more privacy when desired; both could face each other in the morning after being fully awakened and much more becoming – and both could spend the evening in the same room when both consented. COMMENTS PLEASE.

I want to see you before I see anyone else. I don't know what time I will be arriving in Chicago, but whatever time it is, I will come to your house first. Do you have an extra key to your apartment? If so, could you send it to me – and if not, could you leave it somewhere that I could obtain it without letting the entire family know that I have returned? I want very much to see you before I see anyone else. The key will permit me to remain at your apartment in the event I return when you are still at work.

I only hope that I am able to leave the Army when my tour of duty is completed. There has been a great deal of rumor about placing a "freeze" upon all active duty personnel. I usually don't pay much heed to rumors, but this one is so frightening that it really bothers me. If President Johnson decides to extend all military personnel, it would mean at least another year in the Army for me. Just the thought gives me the chills. If you have any influence with a couple of saints, have them throw in a few good words for us.

You won't be receiving a letter from me for awhile. Henry, Cheryl and I will be leaving for a week's tour of Spain. I don't know how it's going to turn out – right now it's rather cold here – but we're hoping for the best. Of course, I'll send postcards – and take pictures (did you ever see a Spanish duck?) – and tell you all about it when I return, which should be March 10th – which should make it – provided nothing goes wrong – only 28 days until I depart for you – and the States.

I want to write more, Klunkie, because I don't feel lonely anymore and I want to talk to you, but it's already 11:30 pm and I have a long day ahead of me tomorrow – the auditors are coming Monday and I have a great deal of statistics to compile.

I must go.

How I Miss You
Dennis

I pray this ongoing troop buildup in Vietnam isn't going to impact my April discharge. The Tet Offensive last month contradicted President Johnson's message that we're winning the war and there's "a light at the end of the tunnel." This can't be happening! Not now, when I'm so close to going home—this close to being with Maggie.

March 13, 1968

My Dearest Dennis,

I must apologize for not writing sooner. I am so glad that you wanted to see me first. It's going to be very difficult once you're home. You'll have so much to do (unpacking, arranging, setting plans etc.) and I know you'll be swooped up by relatives and friends, that I'm very happy that we'll have a few moments alone untouched by clock watching and telephone calls.

Separate bedrooms? Well, I think that if I woke up during the night feeling afraid, I'd want a comforting hand right near me. And if rollers turn my husband off when we're making love, then I'll wait until he's fast asleep before I set my hair. And I'll eat a Cert before he awakes to my first kiss. And if we need privacy there's a den, or a long drive, or a lonely walk. No, separate bedrooms may be a great solution to some people's lull in romance, but not for Miss Maggathie. If my husband loses his interest because of the monotony of it all, I won't be Maggathie!! My husband wouldn't even suggest separate bedrooms (or I'd cry to death).

Did I tell you that Patsy and Leo are building a new home? Well, my dad is going with them when they move. That means Miss Maggathie will be soloing it for real! I can laugh about it now, but the thought of it sometimes actually frightens me. Guess I'm not so grown up after all.

I received two threatening phone calls within the last week. I'm not sure if the caller (a male) is a genuine lunatic or some screwball pulling a not-so-funny-funny. I've got people working on it though.

So, how was Spain?

Thank you for explaining your decision on to be a captain or not to be. I was very worried that you may be making a mistake. Now I'm certain that you haven't

Do you see that? Someone blew a horn outside and I jumped about 15 feet! Silly Maggathie.

I think I'm going to end this and get to bed. It's a spring-like rainy night perfect for cuddling --- my pillow? I'll write again as soon as possible.

With love,
Maggathie

CHAPTER 22

COMING HOME

Around 15 March 1968

My Dear Miss Maggathie:

I finally have a chance to sit down and write you a letter. Things have really been piling up since my return from Spain and even now I have little time to write. Since I will be departing Germany in three more weeks and giving my position to the officer who succeeds me, I have a great deal of partially finished projects to complete. This has kept me busy a vast majority of the time. I'm sorry I couldn't write sooner.

My trip to Spain was a worthwhile experience. In capsule, we were almost run off the road by three French teenagers; we saw a bull fight our first day in Spain; our plane to the island of Majorca was lightly struck by lightning; and I lost my friend's camera. The last episode promptly curtailed my spending as I will have to pay about $60.00 for the lost item.

I would like to tell you more about my trip to Spain, but I really don't have the time. No pictures either.

The days are steadily progressing and I'm still keeping my fingers crossed. With Westmorland asking for 200,000 more soldiers, 23 days still looks mighty far away. Why don't you put in a few good words for us to the Blessed Mother.

As for "Mes," well, how could you help but fall in love with him. But just be careful, Klunkie. If you give too great a part of your heart to him, I'll have to inform the proper authorities that he entered the country illegally.

And of course he met "Benjie." It was that damn fool octopus that mentioned your name to him in the first place. You didn't think I'd risk telling him about you if I ever had any hopes of keeping him with me. Once "Benjie" spilled the beans though, it would have been foolish of me to remain silent.

Klunkie, I want you to know that I miss you. I want you to know this because I probably won't be writing too often in the next three weeks. I have a great deal to do here yet. I just don't want you thinking that my silence implies indifference. I know how pessimistic you are regarding our relationship and I don't want unavoidable circumstances to prompt you to conclude wrongly.

I must go now, Klunkie.

Missing You
Dennis

P.S. What flavor ice cream was that that you dribbled down your bosses window?
P.P.S. No, I don't swallow my gum. I found that if you stick it behind your ear, it can be rechewed for as long as nine days.

March 17, 1968

My Dearest Dennis,

I've so much to say to you and yet I'm afraid that you may not want to hear it.

First of all, I miss you so very much. I've needed you so badly these past few weeks. Everything is finally working itself out somehow. Be ready to hear all about the terrible times of troubled Klunkie someday. I don't wish to waste time now on a subject so very uninteresting.

Prepare yourself for a lot of loving-up once you're home. I think I'll just love you to death when I see you. I won't maul you or anything as aggressive as that -- or will I? No, I have so much to say to you.

I'm so excited. D-day is only 26 days away unless old LBJ sticks his nose into the situation.

Please don't expect to see too many changes around here. In spite of my exercising, I still look like a mud fence. In spite of the extra money I'm making, this 2x4 apartment looks like a 2x4 apartment.

I hope you miss me.

I love you, Dennis. And sometimes even when the hope of finding your love seems to grow dim, I think that perhaps I'm only imagining defeat and that your time to love just hasn't come yet. Then I can go on hoping.

And I love you. And I need your tenderness so very much. I long for your nearness all the day --- and night.

With Love,
Maggathie

March 19, 1968

My Dearest Dennis,

I only have a little time to write as I am already at work and must start within the hour.

Nothing really exciting or new has happened to me. At the christening Sunday, I learned to jump rope again, not to mention all the new songs that our next generation knows. (My nieces really kept me hopping -- high heels and all!)

The ice cream cone I so neatly smeared over my boss's car was originally a rainbow cone, but I was down to the chocolate before I decided to throw it away.

Of course I'll mind if I won't hear from you too often for the next few weeks. I certainly will have pessimistic outlooks on our future; I'll probably doubt you; I'll probably worry, but deep down inside I'll know that you want to write, that our future holds only what we can want it to. I'll feel that you miss me, and my worry will vanish when I can hold you again.

Mes hasn't stolen my heart away from you. I almost fell into his trap, but I began to come to my senses when he decided that he looks good with flowers in his hair. My father would kill me if he saw that I was considering a future with a flower child!

Now I really must go as my boss walked in -- into the wall! -- and now demands coffee. (I got him coffee, but I still must go). Sometimes I wonder if that guy isn't still a baby!!

I miss you very much and hope that I'll hear from you as often as you can afford to write. Good luck on your projects, but please don't lose too much sleep over them.

I'll write soon.

Loving you,
Maggathie

March 20, 1968

My Dearest Dennis,

I'm afraid I can't send you a key until my next letter as I gave my spare key to my landlady. We had an emergency here and I was called home from work because she didn't have the key to let the gas company into my apartment. So, I decided to simply have more made. You'll get it though – I promise.

Sometimes I picture what it will be like if you surprise me when you come to Chicago.

At night – I'd be sleeping soundly and awaken with the touch of strong arms and a gentle kiss.

After work – I'd be rushing up the stairway, open the door, and suddenly be caught up in your arms.

In the evening -- I'd be doing something (sewing), suddenly I hear something – turn -- and you're there.

What will happen --

I'll rush to your arms and trip on the way knocking you over -- I'm so Klunkie!!

I miss you very much.

Miss me if you like. Write when you can. I love you.

With love,
Maggathie

P.S. Forgive me for I am sloppy.

Late March 1968

My Dear Miss Maggathie:

At least you know now that I was telling the truth when I said I wouldn't be able to write too often in the next few weeks. I'm sorry I couldn't write sooner, but too many things have been happening. Work of course – but not all work. Since my departure is nearing, a number of my friends have been asking me over their home for supper or throwing small parties in my honor. Add to this such events as – doing some last minute shopping, packing up my property to be shipped, taking my car 300 miles to the harbor to be shipped etc. etc. Please forgive.

Last week-end John Weems and myself took my car to Bremerhaven, Germany to be shipped back to the States. Let me say one thing – it wasn't a pleasant trip. Because of weather conditions – a constant, heavy rain, it took us nine hours to travel 300 miles. We departed Heidelberg at 7:00 pm and arrived in Bremerhaven, somewhat bedraggled, at 4:00 am. Up the next morning – or should I say the same morning – at 8:30 and off to the shipping company. Handed in my car then had to take an eight hour train ride back to Heidelberg. For some strange reason, I was tired for the next two days.

I'm listening to a Bobby Darin album while writing. I think I've made a new discovery. He has a far different style now than in the past. His songs are slow and soft with a touch of folk sound. I think I'll be buying a couple of his albums.

I'm afraid I'm going to have to end now. It's four in the afternoon and I'm due for dinner at Henry and Cheryl's house soon. They've invited a couple more friends over for one of our last meals together.

Forgive me if I really haven't said too much in this letter or recent past ones. Don't assume that something is wrong. I've simply been pressed for time and have found it extremely difficult to concentrate enough to say anything of import. I'll make up for it when I'm home.

I'm going to be extremely pressed for time within the next two weeks – so please understand if there's an unusual long time between letters.

Missing you
Dennis

March 26, 1968

Hi lovey,

Would you believe I'm depressed? I've always known that I'm a demanding -- not demanding --- possessive woman, but now I'm even more certain of the intensity of these feelings. I was thinking of when you'll be home and how much I'm going to want you near me. I'm afraid things will be terrible until I can understand that you cannot always be as close to me as the next room. Oh, but I miss you so very much and how I long to be a part of your everyday life. Like tonight – it's storming and I'm so afraid -- ever since I was hit by lightening last summer. I need you now.

Problems at work have begun to iron out, but now I see new ones erupting. I've been used carelessly as a scapegoat and it is now too late to defend my innocence. I must grow thicker skin.

Patsy is still hanging on and for that reason I'm babysitting tomorrow so that she can go to the doctor. I hope she holds out for at least one more week. I ordered a gown and a matching robe for her to take to the hospital and it hasn't arrived yet.

The days seem to be dragging! You're probably so busy that they're buzzing by for you. I just hope you're not overdoing yourself with your projects. I miss you so very much.

You'll be home around April 12th -- right? It's just like me to get everything goofed up. I was going to suggest meeting you in New Jersey, but I figured you could not give me a definite time. It would be fun though -- driving together all the way -- like in the movies?

Oh Dennis, I must go now. I still must take a bath and set my hair. How I pray that I'll hear from you tomorrow.

Loving you,
Maggathie

P.S. I'm sleepy
P.P. S. I'm afraid of the storm!

March 28, 1968

My Dearest Dennis,

Do you realize that sometime next week I'll be writing my very last letter to you -- at least until you're here in the U.S. I miss you so much.

I received a letter from you on Tuesday and was quite surprised at the length of it. I expected a one paragraph set up with an X marking the signature. I'm certain that nothing is wrong and that you really are busy, but I'm anxious to find how you're going to make up for this when you come home.

I'm at work now so I don't have too much time to write.

You know, I really enjoy writing letters -- especially to you, but I must add that this is one correspondence I'll be glad to see end. How I pray that being with you, near you, from now on will prove to come true and grow into something a million times stronger than that which grew via air mail.

Oh, I must go now. My boss has just asked if I can complete my reports today.

I must go. I love you (I think?)

Maggathie

P.S. I think I really do.

Around 1 April 1968

My Dear Miss Maggathie:

This will probably be another short letter with little to say. I have so many things to do yet that I find it difficult to sit still for more than fifteen minutes.

The packers will be coming tomorrow morning to crate up my household goods. This afternoon I'm going to have to make a complete inventory of everything I own and have everything neatly piled in one room. Unless this is done, I can expect little cooperation from the packers.

You don't have everything all goofed up; I should be home somewhere around the 12th of April. You are right about the time though – it has been flying for me. In two weeks. I've had two free nights. The rest have been filled with dinner engagements and moderate parties.

I'm really going to be sorry to leave some of the friends I've made here. It's really at times like this that I know why I never considered the Army as a career. Of course, if I wasn't in the Army I would never have met them, but somehow that doesn't ease the pain.

I hope to continue corresponding with them, but I know how these aspirations usually end up. One of the parties takes a little longer to answer a letter, then the other takes a little longer to answer the answer – and so on – until neither person is writing anymore. Maybe not in this case though.

That suggestion you made about meeting me in New Jersey – funny, but I had the same idea, and I also arrived at the same conclusion. I know approximately when I'll be arriving in New Jersey – if my plane leaves when scheduled – but I don't know how long it will take for me to be processed out of the Army. If I could even estimate – I would ask you, but I can't even do that.

Klunkie, I'm anxious to see you. I don't know when I'll be arriving in Chicago, but no matter what the time, I'll be coming to you first. If you're at work, you may return home and find me calmly sitting at your kitchen table. If you're home and awake, you may be startled by what appears to be the sound of an opening door. If you're asleep in bed – well – er – uh – are you a sound sleeper?

One more week and I leave Germany.

Very Affectionately
Dennis

April 1, 1968

Dear Dennis,

This will be my last letter to you as I am not certain as to when you'll be leaving Germany. Your homecoming is 11 days away, yet I feel the butterflies on my insides already (either that or I've got worms!)

Patsy had a baby boy, Danny. I'm so happy she had a boy! Your mother has taken charge of the other three with the exception of last Saturday morning when Patsy felt the urge. Tomorrow night I plan to go there and try to catch up on some of the washing and ironing.

I've been doing so much lately that I've barely had time for my routine work. Would you believe I've got homework from work? Ugh.

Oh, I bought a parakeet and his name is Skootie. He's real cute and just as stupid.

My dad is sick. It's nothing too serious but I only wish he would go to a doctor. I suspect arthritis as he has pain in his right arm and leg. I still wish he'd go to a doctor. He's supposed to move sometime next month. I wonder how this will work out.

I'm in such good spirits knowing that you'll be home. Even today, I can barely keep my eyes open but I'm in the mood to sing, or dance, or both.

You don't know how very much I live for the day when you'll click into my apartment. Nothing else matters half as much as when I'll be with you again.

Until I see you, I'll be waiting here thinking of you.

I wonder if I'll miss writing to you.

With love,
Maggathie

CHAPTER 23

THE BEGINNING

I was discharged from the Army on 10 April 1968. After returning to Chicago, I accepted a position in the Personnel Department at Spiegel on 35th and Morgan, while awaiting a response to my applications to the graduate social work programs at Loyola University and University of Chicago. Maggie still works at Gossard Lingerie. From the day I returned home, Maggie and I have been inseparable. With the exception of our time at work, we spend almost every waking minute with each other. Our family and friends have quickly learned their status on our priority list.

I'm now sure that Maggie is the woman I want to marry. Although I realize she's hoping for an engagement ring on her twentieth birthday, I decide against proposing on that day. Knowing Maggie still doesn't fully believe our relationship could lead to marriage, I'm sure she will conclude the engagement isn't going to happen this year, and maybe never. But to propose to Maggie on her birthday would be my asking her to accept me as my gift to her. And that's not how I see it. Wednesday, July 3, 1968, comes and goes without even a hint of a ring.

I want to propose to Maggie on my birthday in August. I'm sure she won't be expecting it and by doing so, I will be asking her to accept my proposal as her gift to me. And she's my gift far more than I am hers.

On Wednesday, August 21, 1968, Maggie and I plan to celebrate my birthday at my brother Leo's new house. I inform her that prior to going there, we have to pick up my parents to drive them to the party. We enter my parents' house up the back porch stairs that lead to the kitchen. As I open the door, the kitchen looks like it would any other day. Directly in front of and perpendicular to the wall is a gray Formica kitchen table with chrome legs and two gray vinyl upholstered chrome-legged chairs on either side. To the left is a short hallway that leads to the front room, and to the right, a walk-in pantry with the always-opened, half-window door. The light gray speckled linoleum floor is worn in familiar places and spotless from almost daily scrubbing, while the walls are a pale yellow from frequent washing. The entire kitchen smells of Pine-Sol and is cleaner than most operating rooms in the finest hospitals.

The house seems empty and Maggie immediately asks where my parents are. Although I know they're already at my brother's house, I tell her they're probably in the front room. Maggie slowly walks down the short hallway, cautiously peering ahead in anticipation of seeing them sitting on the couch. With her back turned to me, I quickly reach into the right pocket of my pants and nervously fumble for the tiny black felt box. My hands are so shaky, I almost drop it as it catches on the upper edge of my pocket. I quickly gather myself and pull it completely out, almost dropping it again. Hurriedly opening the box to display the diamond ring, I softly whisper, "Maggie."

Maggie pauses and slowly turns her head to my whisper. Upon looking back, she glances down at my hands. Then her eyes dart from the ring in my right hand, to my face, then back to my hand again. Her face is ashen as she turns fully toward me.

Then I quietly say what I have never said to any woman before, "I love you."

Maggie knows the full meaning of these three words:

> "When I say "I love you," it will mean I want you for my wife; I want you to be the mother of my children; I want you to stand by my side as long as life permits. It will mean that you are the one who complements me, who makes me whole. When I say "I love you," it will mean that my life is yours. Everything I do, everything I hope to do, all my wildest dreams, all my fondest desires are for you. When I say "I love you," it will mean that there is no other and far more important, that there will be no other."

Maggie continues staring up at me, then down at the ring, then up again. Her hands shake as she quickly brings them to her lips. Her eyes cover half her face and glisten with tears. Suddenly she screams. She grabs the ring from my outstretched hand, box and all, and screaming and crying, runs around the kitchen table into the pantry, slamming the door behind her. I wait, expecting Maggie to soon emerge after composing herself. Twenty seconds pass and the door remains shut.

I walk to the pantry door and look through the window. Maggie is sitting on the floor in the right-hand corner, under the shelves of canned foods, legs pulled tight to her chest, her head buried in her knees—sobbing. As I slowly open the door, she looks up at me, tears streaming down her face. I gently lift her to her feet and hold her tight in my arms.

We both stand there—trembling.

Maggie and I marry one year later, on August 24, 1969.

Our journey is just beginning.

CPSIA information can be obtained
at www.ICGtesting.com
Printed in the USA
FFOW01n1825281014
8415FF